The Zymoglyphic Anthology

Volume II

INTRODUCTION

This second volume of compilations and selections continues to reflect the dual nature of the museum's work, both creation and curation, looking inward and also reaching outward.

The first volume had a singular focus: the museum. One section was a compilation of documents that had been issued by the museum over the years. The "Orbital Views" section collected essays, literature, and art about or inspired by the museum

In this volume, the museum section is retained, but the focus is on the creative community that has welcomed the museum and its curator during its relatively brief time in Portland. The works that have been selected (both verbal and visual) are not necessarily about the museum, but instead have been selected for relevance to the general themes of the museum. One of those themes is the ways in which creative people tap into the their sources of inspiration. These contributions represent a variety of paths from divine inspiration and dreams to alchemy, mythic archetypes, spontaneous drawing, and surrealist techniques.

Jim Stewart
Editor
Curator of the Zymoglyphic Museum

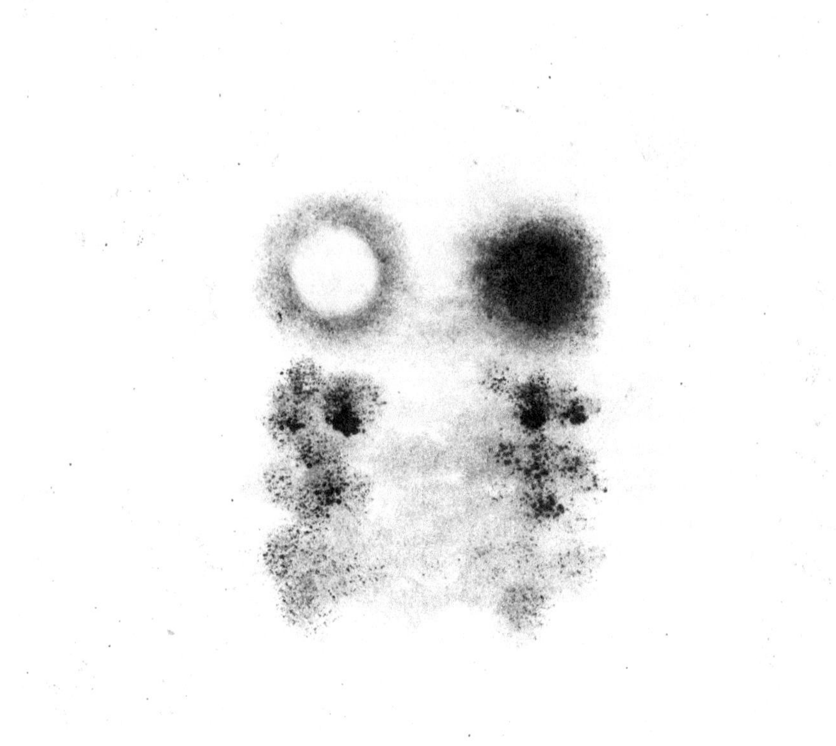

Navigate beyond the veil of yourself alone...Split yourself in two.

-- Coleman Stevenson

Contents

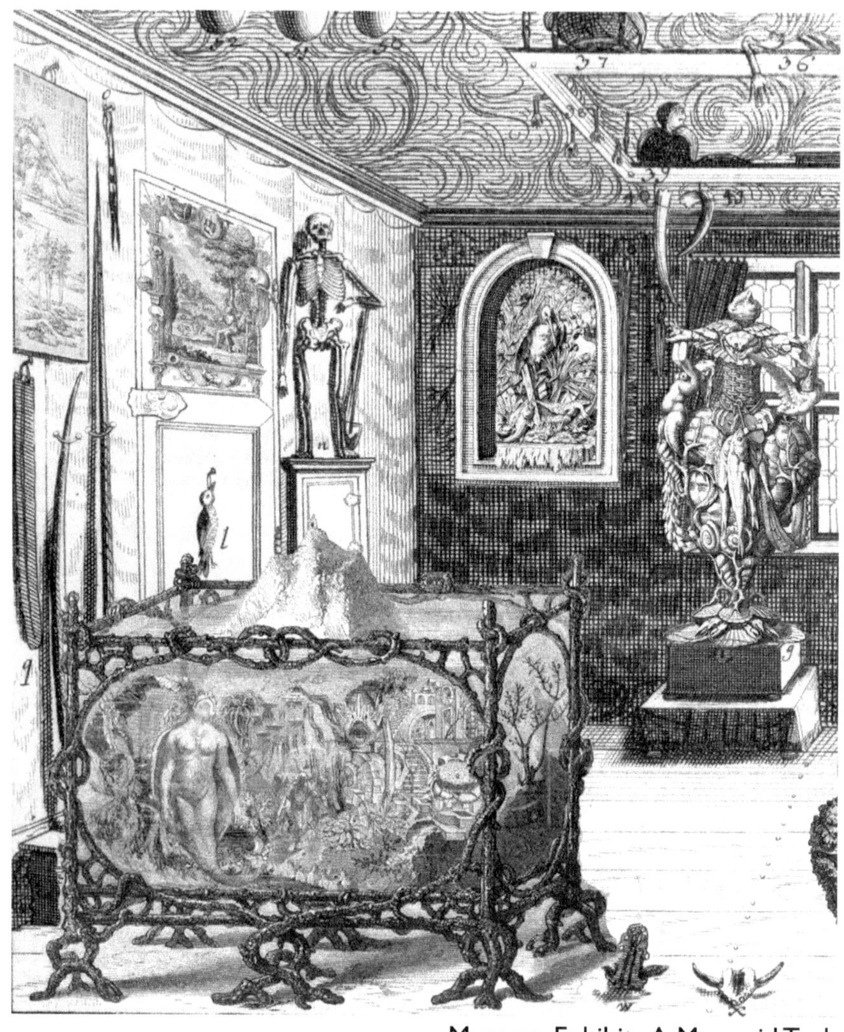

Museum Exhibit: A Mermaid Tank

1. The Museum

If I had the nose to live in the dust, the General would not be me who would then complain about the ecology and everything possible to speculate and involuntary, so this is my favorite aquarium. Only one club tent in the middle, no glattgeschliff'nes glass, brown algae covers in just outside. And then it would dawn and gush to the ceiling.

from a now-vanished German blog entry about the museum's parlor aquarium, via Google translation

THE CURATOR'S TALE, PART 2

Recap of Part 1 (1950-2006)

The original Curator's Tale was written in 2006 for the museum's website (as "How the Museum Came to Be"). The story was reprinted in the first volume of the Zymoglyphic Anthology as "The Curator's Tale, Part I." It chronicled the development of the museum from a childhood collection of rocks, shells, beach finds, and Indian implements to assemblages of natural and rusty objects, and then to surreal dioramas, faux artifacts, and eventually a narrative context for it all.

Most people, including myself, assumed I would be a scientist when I grew up. This idea soon became problematic because science requires specialization and I found all its fields, from subatomic physics to ecology and sociology, interesting. Even all of science wasn't enough. I needed to include the arts as well, an element of creativity and imagination to complement the admittedly amazing but still bounded realm of empirical reality. Being an artist ultimately came to the rescue by offering an approach where I could synthesize anything, the more creative the better, rather than having to stick to literal facts.

The concept of a personal museum, particularly one from a parallel dimension, evolved from that mix as a way to accommodate and structure all the math, science, creativity, and literature that I wanted to pack into it.

We backtrack a bit to begin Part 2 at the dawn of the new millennium. After existing as scattered constructions in the house for a number of years, the museum now has its own little building, an 8x12 shed which huddles in the driveway of a suburban cul-de-sac. Its rusty hinges swing open once or twice a year to welcome guests during the Open Studios event, attracting maybe 20 or 30 visitors a year. I continue to assemble beach finds and other detritus into assemblages in a crowded garage workshop.

In a way, this isolation probably contributed to making the museum unique. I had no expectation that what I created would be profitable or validated by the art world. My main motivation was really self-discovery, an effort to externalize an inner mythos. I liked the idea of creating scenes and artifacts that were dreamlike but also made of physical objects, as opposed to, say, painting, drawing, or writing about a fantasy world.

But I also did enjoy having people come by, after I got over an initial anxiety about showing the work. I wanted to find and connect with like-minded people, who were few and far between in both my work and non-work environments. Along came the Internet, which at that time was a rich mix of obsessive people with niche interests. In 2001, I acquired the zymoglyphic.org domain and set up a Web site documenting the museum's exhibits. The site was divided into Dioramas, Artifacts, Orientalia, and Curiosities. Its modest summary read:

"The museum consists of a number of miniature dioramas and a collection of interesting curiosities which have been assembled to illuminate some of the more obscure reaches of the imagination."

It wasn't until five years later that the museum identified the currently accepted division of Zymoglyphic history into four ages. The Rust Age exhibit gathered the various artifacts that were loosely inspired by indigenous art and associated them with an imagined mythical culture. The Age of Wonder was based on a mix of Renaissance curiosity cabinets and 19th century natural history museums, whose dioramas were given a surrealist twist. The Era of Oriental Influence in a sense plays off the European fascination with the Orient, but really results from my own fascination with the way Asian cultures use nature in art (tray landscapes, bonsai, ikebana, viewing stones, and so forth) without really calling it "art." The Modern Age started as a sort of parody of modern art and became a catch-all for things that didn't fit elsewhere. I made no attempt to develop a detailed backstory beyond those basic concepts.

The museum's blog debuted late in 2005, and 2006 was a peak year for blogging. I used the blog for announcements, reports on places, events, and artists that I considered zymoglyphic, and short personal essays. The format was to have at least one striking image at the top, followed by some literary prose making interesting connections about relevant topics. I spent a lot of weekends wordsmithing and link-checking my posts. The blog was updated weekly for a while, then monthly, then once or twice a year. The attrition was mostly due to lack of response.

A proliferation of media

My natural medium is spontaneous assemblage, particularly of natural (or weathered artificial) objects. I like to find objects that have potential, often something that does not look like what it actually is. I arrange my finds in three-dimensional space, moving them around until they "glow." I'm happy with this process and generally not interested in learning any techniques or practicing to make perfect.

However, my first blog entry was an announcement of a set of acrylic paintings that came out of a class I had attended. I was essentially laying out acrylic paint and water on masonite held flat, then swishing it around as the pigment settles, often in complex branchy patterns. I made six of them that I really liked.

Some years later I decided to try spontaneous drawing, starting with a blank sheet of paper, making some random marks, then filling in with whatever came to mind. Invariably they turned out to be surrealist landscapes. I created about 20 of them that I liked over the course of a few months. The inspiration dried up after that, but I liked the good ones enough to publish them as a book.

Another year I got inspired to create collages from old engravings. I created a few dozen of them in Photoshop over the course of a year or so. Being digital, they can be printed out easily and indefinitely. I have never believed in the idea of limited editions. I think if someone enjoys the images, they should be able to have one. I sell the prints in the museum shop and they have proven to be very popular over the years. I still get a thrill from the idea of someone framing one and hanging it on their wall.

I had always been fascinated by animation, whether stop-motion, hand-drawn, or computer-generated, but I did not have the patience to actually create one. I discovered that the Photoshop layers that made up the collages could be fed into software that would allow you to move them around and fly a virtual camera through the resulting landscape. The result is now a Modern Age exhibit.

More digital magic! My father, a dedicated do-it-yourselfer, self-published a wildflower guide in the pre-digital era. This involved meticulous film photography, large production runs, and driving to bookstores to fulfill orders. Nowadays a book can all be laid out on a computer, uploaded to a printing company, and exactly however many books you needed would show up on your doorstep. My first publication, in 2010, was "the museum in a book"—photographs of the artifacts, exhibits, and collections. Soon after, I created books from the collage prints and the drawings. As with the prints, I am excited when people buy the books. I like the thought of them sitting on someone's library shelf, perhaps retrieved on occasion for reference or inspiration.

Yet another medium presented itself when my wife created a postcard for the museum. I got inspired and created a dozen more. You can take them as little works of mail art or just souvenirs of an interesting place you have visited. Like physical books, I liked the idea of these little missives working their way through the delivery system, sent by someone who had to put on a stamp and mail it.

Postage stamps have always been a part of my collections along with the various natural objects. In a way, they don't seem to fit. As a child, my collection was focused on exotic places, and the idea of a microcosm that encapsulated the whole world. Later I added stamps from made up countries. I liked that they seemed to be physical manifestations of imaginary regions. Once the notion of a Zymoglyphic region existed, it seemed just logical to design and issue a few postage stamps for it!

The Great Transition - On to Portland!

The San Mateo version of the museum trundled along for a few years in the early twenty-teens, continuing the Open Studios tradition and hosting a few other events. I added a little museum shop to sell books, prints, and postcards. I took to the road to sell a few books and prints, gave a talk at the local Obscura Society, had some sketchers come through.

The museum closed without fanfare in May of 2014, after its last Open Studios event. I retired in January of that year and we moved to Portland in July. I immediately took to it. It seemed a mossy garden of Eden, soaked by nourishing rain and gray skies, harboring a bumper crop of creatives and sympathetic institutions. There were people who wanted to hang out in cafes and pubs to talk about art, literature, and philosophy instead of TV programs, sports, and stock prices. There were people with grand but personal creative projects. I was especially drawn to the Faux Museum (now gone), Curious Gallery (discontinued), and the Kayak Museum (still going strong).

I tried to set up a temporary mini-museum in an appropriately leaky and rundown detached garage of the place we were renting, but it did not go well. I ended up moving it to a rented studio in Portland's Eastside Industrial district. I devoted some of the new space to a gallery showing other people's work.

My career as a gallery owner was short-lived, however. I did not actually want to run a gallery, having to judge other people's work, and dealing with organizing openings. Besides, I had a new space to set up.

The new museum opens to great acclaim!

We finally purchased a home in May of 2016 with a two-story detached garage that became the museum's new location. I transported the remaining exhibits from San Mateo and the temporary location to the new place and created some new exhibits. The new museum opened without fanfare and greeted its first visitors on November 17, 2016. More people visited in the first few months than in the whole 14 years in the Bay Area. The local alternative weekly listed it in their "Best of Portland" issue of 2017.

2018 was a banner year in many ways. In the spring, a high school student in Florida had become enamored of the museum via its website. He flew out with his mother to film a mini-

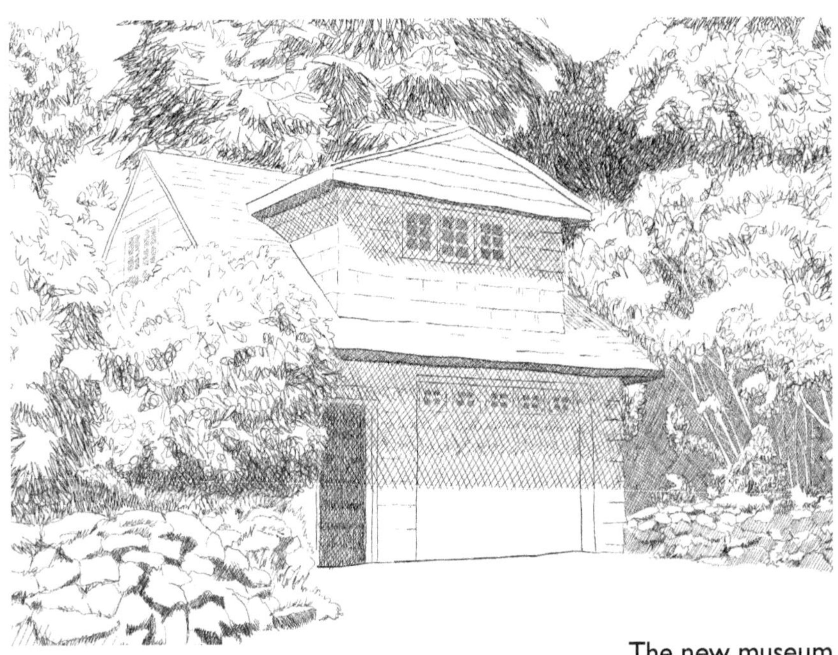

The new museum

documentary about the museum. In March, Atlas Obscura sponsored a Zymoglyphic-themed mushroom tasting at the museum. A seven year old girl visited late that year and wrote a "Kid's Guide to the Museum," still one of the museum's most popular publications. The museum was written up on the local glossy lifestyle monthly, the neighborhood high school newspaper, and an in-flight airline magazine. Five star reviews proliferated on social media. Blog entries were made. Locals and tourists alike declared "I love that place!"

One day, Feb. 11, 2018 to be exact, a Facebook posting announcing the open day showed 57 people going and 574 interested. It had a "reach" of 17,000. 124 people showed up that day and it was very unpleasant. I wanted to shut the door and lock it; I got flustered with so many people wanting my attention to buy something or ask a question. I stopped doing any active publicity after that. I got the museum removed from a popular list of "things to do with kids." To date, I have turned down three requests from local TV stations wanting to do stories featuring the museum.

I still welcome attention from bloggers, print publications, scholars, and any genuine enthusiast who has been to the museum and wants to write about it. Photography is encouraged and has resulted in lots of great photos on social media. I especially welcome those inspired to create works of art based on the museum.

The sort of inspired attention the museum garnered in 2018 fell off abruptly after January of the following year. There was still a steady stream of visitors, many enthusiastic, but few spontaneous projects coming out of it.

Books

I declared 2019 the year of the book(s)! Just as the museum's internet presence was an attempt to reach beyond the geographical borders of the physical museum, so I saw books as a way to reach across time as perhaps the most durable storage medium short of clay tablets. I also thought it would be fun to add book publisher to my retirement resume. Books appeal to me as compact repositories of knowledge, images, wisdom, and even world view. They are a nice, solid compromise between the ungainly, fragile physical presence of the museum and its insubstantial doppelganger on the internet.

The first book out of the chute was a collaboration of sorts. A friend and writer whose style I admire was in need of some work, so I commissioned him to write a book in August of 2019. It was to be zymoglyphic-themed but otherwise I gave him no specific direction. The result, *Hotel Zymoglyphic* by Jason Squamata, was not at all what I had expected - a loosely connected set of poems instead of an extended prose piece. It has turned out well, however; it's a book I can dip into over and over, rather than read once and be done. It even came with a spoken word version that added a whole new dimension to it.

The second book that year was *The Zymoglyphic Anthology*. I had printed up a lot of brochures over the years and they were taking over the museum shop, so I thought I would compile them into a single volume. I added in some historical documents, and recruited essays and zymo-based fiction, to create a wildly eclectic assemblage of documentation.

Book three is an update to the original guide to the museum, which had not been updated since it was first published in 2010. This volume is intended to be the museum in book form, a documentation of two decades worth of developing one idea in all its ramifications. It actually avoids reference to the museum as a physical location, implying that the museum itself may be a fictional construct.

The latest book, of course, is the one you are holding now. It's an organic thing, partly a repository for any essays or other writing that I do, and partly a way to connect with and encourage others to share their perspectives on the museum project.

As much as I enjoy the processing of designing and creating books, I'm not much for the sales and marketing side, so the number of books sold tends to be quite small. I generally get little if any feedback, especially compared to the physical museum. It becomes an act of faith to believe that these works are inspiring a select host of congregants and impressionable minds.

The plague hits

My ambivalence about the museum as a destination for "oddity tourism" was resolved in March of 2020 at the beginning of the international contagion that shut down all local cultural institutions as "non-essential." It remains to be seen at press time whether this is temporary or permanent.

The last visitor to the museum the last open day (March 8) was the travel editor of the local newspaper which was (finally) doing an article on weird museums in Portland. He was visitor number 3,600. It struck me that the museum is an art project that gets covered by a travel reporter rather than an art or cultural reporter.

The museum returns to the isolation from which it came.

INTERVIEW WITH THE CURATOR

A wide-ranging, five part self-interview by and with the curator of the Zymoglyphic Museum. This interview was conducted shortly before and during the museum's pandemic-induced hiatus in the spring of 2020. Much of it was done sitting in a cozy chair with a lap robe or a cat, drinking strong black tea and looking out on the grey Portland rain.

1. MUSEUM AS DESTINATION: VISITING THE MUSEUM

Q: What kind of people have come to visit the museum?

Visitors vary in what they know about the museum before they visit. There are people who are just passing by and see the sign, or, more likely, who saw the name pop up on a map app and were curious about it. According to Google, "museums near me" is a common search term that leads to the museum's website. Some look around for a while, say "thank you" or ask a token question, then leave. Others are amazed that such a thing exists and that they stumbled on to it. If they are visitors who happen to be in town on the rare day that the museum is open, they often have a special feeling that they were meant to discover it.

I get a lot of tourists visiting Portland who are looking for a typically Portland experience. In New York, you go to a Broadway play; in Portland, you visit a quirky museum. The museum is on a lot of lists of off-the-beaten-path Portland attractions. It gets glowing reviews on social media, which will attract people even if they know nothing else about it.

There is a subset of tourists who seek out the unusual wherever they go, such as little museums and roadside attractions. I call this "oddity tourism" and would certainly place myself in that category.

A more specific group would be those who are interested in the particular themes of the museum. The backstory and dead things resonate with goths, steampunkers, rogue taxidermists, and rock-and-bone collectors. Others are interested in museology, curiosity cabinets, art made from natural objects, surrealism, and so forth. Often they are other artists (or creative people who don't feel comfortable calling themselves artists) and may get inspired to do something creative with their collections. These are usually the people that I have the most interesting conversations with, and who often become Facebook friends. Some of them come back later to donate things they have and don't know what else to do with. These donations in turn sometimes inspire new exhibits.

Out of the more involved group, a small number, usually local people, become involved with the museum in some ongoing way; those are the people I'm most interesting in attracting. With over 3,000 visitors over the last three years, there have been probably a couple dozen visitors in that category, the one-percenters.

Q: How do people find out about the museum?

The commonest response when I ask people the question is "somewhere on the internet." Often it is the Atlas Obscura website which is the premiere online source for oddity tourism. Others hear about it from friends who have visited; often local people will bring friends and relatives visiting from out of town.

Q: If you want to attract more of the involved people, why aren't you open more often? It seems like lots of people are interested in seeing the museum!

Partly it's not wanting to be tied to a schedule, but I think the real reason is just a personality limitation on my part. While visitors are generally well-behaved, I just get tired of meeting new people and answering the same questions over and over. The questions are of course asked in good faith (although I think that people sometimes feel obligated to ask a few questions), and the asker has no way of knowing that they are the umpteenth person that day to ask that particular question. The stress between my irritation at the questions and the inappropriateness (to me) of such irritation becomes uncomfortable.

Q: What are some examples of repeated questions?

"Are you the artist?" "Did you make all this?"
"How long have you been doing this?" "What got you started?"
"What does 'zyglo-mo-zimmo-morphic mean?"

Q: How do you deal with the questions?

I've pre-preemptively posted signs with the definition of

"zymoglyphic" that I can point to. I have some fairly short stock answers for the others, because I'm not sure whether the questioner really wants to know or is just asking out of politeness.

If I were comfortable being known as a curmudgeon I could put up a sign starting with "Rules: Do not ask about..." or something, but that would be counter to my main goal of connecting with people.

Q: What kinds of responses (other than questions) do you get, and which are best and worst?

I've never had any truly negative complaints, either to my face or within earshot. I suspect that people are simply too polite to say anything negative. I'm the same way myself with other people's work. I'm sure some visitors must be uncomfortable with the subject matter or the lack of craft or some such thing. There are responses which I take as neutral, such as "You must have put a lot of work into this." I don't really see it as work. Another is "thank you for sharing this." I'm not really sure what to make of that one.

Many people call it "weird." They often mean this as "weird in a good way" and I often use the term myself to find things that will interest me. But I also take it as a distancing, as "I don't really get what you're doing here." I generally don't self-identify as weird.

Another common response is "I've never seen anything like this!" This one certainly might be intended at neutral, but I actually like it because I like the idea of doing something no one else is doing. "Awesome" is of course common and appreciated, and "enchanting" is one I particularly like. The generally positive reviews on social media tend to assure me that any enthusiasm is not just performative. The enthusiasm helps keep me going. The response I like best is when someone says it's "inspiring" and that they will get to work on some long-forgotten art project.

Q: Do you ever respond in character, possibly by insisting that some made-up thing is real?

No! I realize that a performance as a character is a potential
dimension that would fit perfectly in the museum context. I could
dress up as a mad scientist and give tours that way. I think the
issue for me is that role-playing creates a barrier between me and
the other person. My goal is to connect with visitors. I'd rather
just have a straightforward discussion, and I think that being
in character would detract from that. I once agreed to be part
of a LARP (live action role-playing) game where people came
to the museum to pick up clues for a role-playing game. It was
not pleasant. It's just not something I'm comfortable doing. I
don't even like being asked what the museum is all about when I
meet someone. Usually, I will just hand someone one of my little
business cards and tell them to check out the website.

Q: So no tours I'm guessing.

No, I would much rather deal with visitors one on one. I
discourage school groups, field trips, and similar groups. This is
partly logistical in that it is a small space, but really I don't want
to be leading a tour and I would rather have people enjoy the
space on their own.

Q: Aren't you really playing a role as "The Curator"?

Yes, it does give me a cover of some sort, just not in person. Most
of my written output is from the point of view of a curator, or
"museum management." This provides me just enough cover for
comfort.

Q: Do you teach classes or do workshops?

No, because I feel that what I do doesn't really involve any specific
techniques that can be taught. I myself learn best by copying and
being inspired rather than being taught, so I'm hoping people will
simply see what's possible and create their own version of it.

Q: Has that ever actually happened?

I did get one email from a visitor from out of town that said he had been inspired to organize his collections into a sort of museum, but mostly my idea that "personal museums are an underutilized mean of creative expression" has not received much traction.

2. MUSEUM AS ART PROJECT: IS IT ART?

Q: You have a survey for visitors that includes the following question:

This is

__ an elderly eccentric with a weird hobby, a spare garage, and too much time on his hands,

__ a complexly layered, fully integrated work of art.

What's the correct answer?

I like to think it's the second one in the guise of the first.

Q: Are you an artist?

In Part 1 of the Curator's Tale I described coming out as an artist despite no formal art training. I'm quite comfortable with the term now.

Q: If this is art, why isn't it in a gallery and for sale to collectors like real art? Is this just a hobby?

This is a particularly annoying question! I think creativity does not equal commerce and commerce in fact often serves to corrupt creativity.

Q: Okay, but why not pursue a career in the art world if you want this project to be validated as art and not just some oddity?

The most practical answer is that the work itself is fragile and ephemeral and I'm not interested in adapting what I do just to make it more archival. I also get attached to what I make and don't really want to let it go. But there are lots more issues.

1. Independence and lack of being judged. I don't have to submit anything to a jury and get turned down, or alter what I do in order to get accepted by a gallery. I have on occasion submitted works to galleries. Generally, if there is a jury involved, the work is not accepted.

2. No competition. By working in my own genre, I'm not competing with anyone else (except maybe the Museum of Jurassic Technology).

3. I think my view of art is fundamentally different from the current art world, which is currently focused on cultural critique. My view of art as creative self-expression is probably considered outdated in the postmodern world.

4. Having a museum provides more personal interaction with people who are interested in what I'm doing than having work in a gallery would.

Q: You could make those collages into limited edition fine art prints.

I'm not willing to make them "framed limited edition giclee prints" just to justify a higher price. I'd rather that anyone who wants one be able to afford it and enjoy it. This is another problem I have with the (visual) art world is the fetishisation of the "one-of-a-kind" which makes it into a collectible and only affordable by the wealthy. Writers and composers don't have this problem—their output can be replicated any number of times with no diminution of perception of quality

Q: So is this outsider art?

I suppose so. I have not had any formal art training. I've taken a few classes here and there but I learn better by osmosis, imitation, and trial-and-error than I do with being taught. I think the results are more creative that way. I try to get an intuitive grasp of basic principles, sometimes through parody or satire.

One advantage of visual art over writing and music is that craft is optional. Outsider art is an entire genre of art devoted to validating the idea that a complete lack of formal training in visual art is no barrier to creating it.

I have consciously avoided the art-school to gallery career path, partly in the perhaps naive conviction that outsider art is more closely connected to a creative wellspring than art which has been rigorously selected for "quality."

On the other hand, I'm not unaware of art history and am consciously creating art within that overall context if not within the system. So I probably fall between the classifications, not an unusual place for me to be.

Q: What other art has influenced you and why?

I find indigenous art inspiring, especially Africa, Oceania, and the art of the American southwest. My father was fascinated with the Hopi Indians and learned traditional dances. I like the idea that compelling imagery is created using natural materials for spiritual use and not as "art."

Similarly, Asian nature-based processes such as Japanese flower arranging, Chinese scholar's rocks and tray landscapes are compelling to me both because of the use of natural materials (still living, in some cases, such as bonsai) and the end goal of creating objects of contemplation, not art per se.

Q: Was there any art world art that appealed to you?

I went to college in New York City in the late 1960s, so I got exposed to a lot of it. I had a friend who was an aspiring art critic (the only one of us who knew what he wanted to be when he grew up). I generally thought classical art, while clearly well-crafted, was rather dull in its content, except for landscapes. I didn't really connect with modern abstraction either, except in an abstract way. I liked the general Dada/Fluxus idea that art could be anything and anything could be art

The style that I really connected with was Surrealism. They pioneered the use of existing materials in art with collage and assemblage, and even the collection and display of found objects in art gallery displays. I also liked the fact that they sought

to create art organically and spontaneously, and that special
meaning could result from juxtaposition of disparate objects and
images.

Q: Why do you like assemblage and collage as media?

It fits my particular approach to things which is to start with
what's presented to me and do something creative with it, rather
than plan something out. A lot of craft, skill, planning, and
training is required in painting and sculpture, not so much in
assemblage. The randomness or synchronicity of objects that are
found at the same time or end up together in a work space often
suggests creative inspirations that would not have occurred to me
otherwise. Using existing objects instead of creating new ones
means that the components retain their original associations.

On a more mundane level, the lack of a predetermined goal
means that the result generally exceeds the goal, reducing the
risk of disappointment. I get a lot of pleasure out of this. By not
applying much learned craftsmanship to the art, I can avoid being
told what to do and just figure it out myself.

Q: Why the preponderance of natural objects in the assemblages?

The natural world is just so inherently interesting. Artificial
objects are usually interesting because of their cultural
connotations, and, to me, they get more interesting if they are
naturally weathered in some way. With natural objects, the detail
just gets better the closer you look at it.

It's also something that goes back to my childhood. Both my
parents were lovers of nature. We hiked and camped a lot. The
whole museum is really my childhood collection of rocks, shells,
and marine life, just grown and branched like an oak from an
acorn.

Q: Why the fascination with decay, skulls, and ugly things as the content of the art?

I grew up in a fairly sterile suburban environment. When I went to New York, I was fascinated by decayed industrial buildings and ruins of all kinds. Anything that has that organic texture added to it I like, whether mold, moss, lichen, rust, fungus, or wherever a primal organic force takes over from a more orderly one.

Besides decay, I find I like things that labeled creepy, weird, or grotesque, such as reptiles, insects, . They just seem more interesting to me than others. Their very alienness suggests new worlds and ways of looking at things.

Also, I've created an environment where I can get people to appreciate the creative potential of things that might otherwise be discarded or overlooked - a leaf, a twig, and possibly me by proxy in some way.

Q: Why museum as a medium?

Most personal-scale museums are single-theme collections, which are interesting, but rather limited. What I'm trying to do here is to expand the concept to create a framework which, like assemblage, creates art from existing objects.

To the extent that you create your own museum contents, a personal museum is an ideal framework for a wildly eclectic body of work.

Q: Most artists who deal with museums as subject matter do so as a cultural critique of the role of museums as taste-makers whose authority needs to be challenged. Are you doing that here?

No, I'm trying to promote the idea that a personal museum is an option for artists who want to work in a variety of media that all have a conceptual unity, rather than creating endless variations of the same concept.

Q: Is there any political content to what you do?

I have consciously avoided any political and pop-culture references in my work, wanting it to have a more archetypal significance. However, looking back on it with a postmodern perspective, I see that it's a fertile ground for discussion of cultural appropriation and colonialism.

 Q: Might this work be considered "subversive" in any way?

I like the idea of subverting the idea of the art gallery. Modern (or contemporary) art is viewed by many as ridiculous or intimidating (depending on their level of confidence), so not presenting this as art has the advantage of attracting people who would never go to a gallery, or an art museum.

Q: You mentioned wanting to separate creativity from commerce. How does money factor in to your work?

I have purposefully separated art from money by having a salable skill that would enable the art to be separate from financial pressures. I do charge for books, prints, and even postcards and brochures, because it indicates to me that the purchaser values it to some degree. I keep prices low so anyone can afford it—books and prints are priced on the order of a cocktail or two, and there are always postcards available for a dollar. I purposely avoid the "limited edition" route of the prints, which artificially inflates the price. I do have a few giveaways, but generally I don't give things away because I imagine people just take anything that's free only to throw it away later.

3. MUSEUM AS SUBJECT: BOOKS AND WRITING

Q: With all the blog verbiage, books, and booklets coming out of the museum, it seems that writing about its various aspects is a major part of your project. Do you consider yourself a writer in addition to being a visual artist? If so, do you ever write about anything else?

Overall I would say no. I used to think that I would like to be a writer. I have some deep mystical notion that getting just the right words down will result in a sort of epiphany. I have bookshelf of classic works from the Homer's Odyssey to Joyce's Ulysses and on into contemporary writers. In college, I mostly hung out with English majors and have generally revered a wider variety of writers than visual artists.

I enjoy the writing process when I am inspired to do it, and it's very satisfying when it comes together. I have on occasion written something that I enjoy reading and rereading. However, the inspiration seems to only come from the museum context. I do like the idea of adding a literary dimension to the visual art.

I have no interest in writing a novel, or learning how to craft plot, dialogue, and character, just as I am not interested in learning to paint or sculpt. I'm more interested in the use of language as a creative medium for expressing ideas in either a straightforward or metaphorical way.

Writing can be useful for organizing and clarifying my own thoughts and recording them for future reference. I do edit as if someone else were reading it, trying to make it flow coherently. I don't get much feedback on the writing (compared to the museum) so it can feel like a waste of time if it's not useful for me.

Q: How does writing compare with creating visual art?

It's a connection to a different, more explicit, but more difficult to capture, wellspring of creativity than visual art. In a practical sense, writing is more portable. You don't need much in the way of physical space or physical objects. With self-publishing, it's easy to distribute your work widely.

Visual art is unique (compared to writing and music) in that you can create something interesting with little to no training, simply by following your intuition. Or I can, anyway. I'm generally pleased with the results that come from a minimal effort in creating a assemblage, for example. Writing takes a lot more work. It requires a specificity that can be left unexpressed in visual art. I work and rework sentences for clarity, trying to find the exact word and even then I'm still not sure. I also take a lot more care with grammar and spelling than I would with whatever the equivalent would be in visual art.

My goal, as with visual art, is to learn something in the process of trying to express, and to connect with others. My learning style is similar to visual art—absorb a lot and let it ferment. With writing I constantly worry if I'm boring the reader, or whether it will get read at all, or if I'm being clear. Even with writing that I like for myself I wonder if anyone else will get it or if I'm being too obscure.

As far as connecting with others, visual art is more accessible in a way. It can be taken in all at once. Writing requires someone to take the time and attention to read through it. This is hard for me because I tend to assume no one is listening or paying attention to what I say. I'm already concerned that this interview is getting way too long and has no pictures.

All that said, I would have to add that writing is easier for me than talking, mostly because I can be spontaneous at first, then correct, rearrange, polish, and discard until I'm happy with it.

Q: So maybe your documentation is more about books than writing.

Yes. My first publications were visual—a book of drawings, a collection of collages, and a guide to the museum that was primarily photographs of the exhibits. The first word-centric book out of the chute had words that were written by someone else. Much of the verbal content of the anthologies is contributed by others.

My book making process is similar to how I create the other parts of the museum—I cobble together a lot of existing parts, get some other people involved, weave various themes together, and arrange it all in a pleasing composition.

Q: You've mentioned that your family environment was more oriented to books than visual art.

My mother was a voracious reader and an aspiring writer. Her ambitions far exceeded her output. Very early on, she wrote an imaginative children's book about tree gnomes and Santa Claus but was unable to get it published. She was also interested in the mystery genre and left behind copious notes with ideas, long lists of potential titles, and bits of dialogue, but no completed works that I could find. We didn't talk about it much, but I gathered from the notes she left behind that much of her interest was using character dialog to talk about ideas.

My father was more interested in science, biology in particular. I don't think he read any literature apart from genre westerns, but he did have lots of natural history texts, field guides, and science books around.

4. MUSEUM AS ALTER EGO: GETTING PERSONAL

Q: So it sounds like you grew up with expectations for yourself around science and literature, then escaped into visual art which was open territory.

Yes. Science was fascinating but too literal and specialized; literature was inspiring but not something I thought I could do well. Art had no expectations for me and I've been able to include aspects of both science and writing into it. Art, for me, combines the discovery aspect of science with a sense of meaning found in literature.

Art was not a main interest of mine when I was growing up, other than some doodling, nor was it a big part of my home environment. By the time I got interested in it, in college, art was "anything you could get way with," as Marshall McLuhan put it at the time. Painting and sculpture were considered passé. This made it very easy for me to accept whatever I did as art.

Q: In your booklet "Creating and Curating Your Own Museum," you say that a personal museum is ideally an instantiation of yourself. Is the museum a sort of alter-ego?

Yes. I think of the museum as a place where I can walk around in a physical representation of my own imagination. I suppose it's basically the same as someone's home decoration, all their choices in furniture, useless objects, wall and yard decorations, and book selection. I've just added a conceptual level to it by giving it an institutional persona.

Q: Are there advantages to having an institutional persona?

The museum also gives me an identity in the community—I'm "that guy with the museum." That works well for me as I'm not comfortable setting up social engagements and often not interested in general socializing, so it's helpful to have a situation where people come to me and who have similar interests.

Having a museum also gives me a way to work with people whose work I connect with. I can collect and display other artists' work, or include their books in the library. With the museum press, I can include their work in anthologies.

Q: Do you create for yourself or for others?

At first, it was just me—a sort of journey into my own imagination and making something concrete out of it. As I've had more visitors, I've enjoyed their enthusiasm and gotten rather addicted to it as an ego boost. A few have even used the words "creative genius."

Q: Do you collaborate with other people?

Sometimes. I find working with others can be both rewarding and frustrating, depending on my expectations. Often I will meet someone and have elaborate fantasies of how they could become involved with the museum. Of course, they often have their own ideas and it usually turns out to be something totally different from what I can imagined. Even working with just myself, I can't predict when I will be inspired and when not.

The museum has worked really well for me as a social magnet. My favorite part of the project has been meeting people who are enthused about and have some of their own creative input. Mostly I pluck them out of the visitor stream. I can look at it through other people's eyes. Both the up and down sides of this are the unpredictability of what other people might do (and, of course, whether they actually follow through on it). It's very satisfying to me to have another pair of eyes and its associated brain look at my work and come up with a creative response.

Q: What do you see as the successes and disappointments so far?

I've created something unique that a lot of people connect with. It's been a good way to pull together a lot of my varied interests in what feels like a constructive and creative way. Having a physical museum been a good way to get my art seen in a world where the supply of art far exceeds the demand (and attention span).

There have been a fair number of creative projects that people have done based on the museum, which is one of my favorite things about it. Some of them I have specifically encouraged, others have been offered spontaneously. The ones I have encouraged often turn out very differently than what I had expected, generally in a good way. I've been pleasantly surprised at how popular the collage prints are and I really enjoy the idea of them hanging on people's walls.

On the other hand, there has not been much of an ongoing community around the museum. I tried to start a Zymoglyphic Society which was great for about a year, but died out due to lack of interest. I suspect that my combination of interests may not overlap with others. If the museum is my alter-ego, then trying to organize people around it is like organizing around a person rather than an idea.

One disappointment is that I meet a lot of local people who seem to be interested in the museum, even enthusiastic, but they very rarely show up to visit.

There have been to date no online reviews of the books or even any real evidence that anyone has read them. This is most likely due to books, whatever the content, being tiny drops lost in a vast sea of words and pictures on paper, which far exceeds the collective attention span. The physical museum by its uniqueness, easily garners eloquent reviews, 5-star ratings, and lots of photos on social media.

I've always had a fantasy that the museum would become the subject of scholarly interest, but that has not happened.

Q: Maybe you should do it yourself!

I actually have done this. My first attempt is included in the first anthology, reviewing the museum using the persona and pseudonym of an imagined scholar. I had an idea that treating the academic journal article as a literary form would be interesting, the ideal merger of science and literature.

Q: Speaking of which, what's the deal with interviewing yourself? Shouldn't someone else be conducting the interview?

I'm not very good at coming up with something on the spot that I'm happy with. I like being able to take my time organizing my responses and rewriting for clarity. So this becomes a way to organize my own thoughts. I had also thought that an interview format would be more engaging for others to read. I carry on a lot of internal dialogue, so it's natural to be talking with myself.

Q: Do you let people other than yourself interview you?

Sure! There are a couple of email interviews linked on the web site, and a friend did one on his esoteric radio program. However, I have turned down several requests from local TV stations, partly to avoid the extra traffic to the museum and partly because I'm just not comfortable being on camera. I would rather be heard than seen.

Q: Is being a curator your actual job?

Yes, in many ways it is the ideal job. I don't have anyone that I need to report to, nor do I have any customers whose needs I'm beholden to. I do feel obligated to have the museum open at the posted hours, and to be a gracious host, but nothing bad would happen if I just closed up.

When I retired, I was struck that my curator job was very much like the old one—mostly working at the computer, taking walks to take a break from it, making lists of tasks & prioritizing them. Even though I had no one to report to, I still felt that I was wasting time if I was not being productive on my project list.

Q: As your own boss, I suppose you have to do your own performance reviews. Anything you would give yourself low marks on?

Sales and marketing, primarily. The physical museum sells itself due to its uniqueness and limited capacity. Book publishing, however, is highly competitive, and I don't want to go to book fairs or do a lot of promotion on the internet, even though I would like for the books to gain a wider audience. I have a blog that I used to enjoy updating, but it's fallen to a low priority in recent years. I haven't really kept up with other social media except to make announcements. I don't really have an improvement plan for any of those areas.

Q: How about things you've done well?

I have lots of skills! I can do the design and layout of the books myself. I enjoy doing the writing, editing, and photography. I have experience in user interface design and can maintain the web site. None of these skills are at the level where I would want to do it for others, but they work well together for the museum as a one-man operation.

5. MUSEUM AS DREAM: LOOKING AHEAD

Q: What are your plans for the future?

My favorite part of this project is how it has grown organically without a plan. The museum concept has provided a protective shelter and a place of honor for projects that might otherwise have had nowhere to go.

In a way, I feel that the museum itself is approaching completion. I've documented it in a book, the website seems close to its final organization, the exhibits seem like a complete unit, the stream of visitors is reliable.

The whole museum framework sometimes feels like a sort of cage to the extent that I feel the need to find a spot in the structure for any new thing that I do. Sometimes the idea of just starting something brand-new and unknown has its appeal. I may need to get back into the proverbial basement and find those neglected aquaria that I dream about.

Nevertheless, I do have quite a few projects in the hopper that I am looking forward to!

Q: What are those projects?

Esoteric Museology is a term I have been using for the study of personal museums. This project could manifest a new book and a web site, and ideally an exhibit and catalog of artifacts from personal museums. This project would promote the idea of personal museums as a means of creative expression.

Creating an alchemy lab is a mad-scientist fantasy that I have. I like the idea of metaphorical chemistry combining my nostalgia for chemistry-set experiments with ancient traditions of exploring esoteric ideas with alchemical implementation.

Q: Any plans for about getting other people involved other than just waiting for someone interesting to show up?

I'm planning a residency program, which would be a good way to connect with like-minded people in a sustained way. Artists could use the museum's resources to create their own takes on zymoglyphia.

Q: As of this moment, the museum has been on hiatus

**for nearly two months due to the pandemic, with no end
in sight. How is that going?**

Not too badly, really. Most of my projects now, such as book
production, are computer based, and I can still go putter around
in the museum whenever it's warm enough. I do miss having
visitors, though.

The physical structure of the museum, the collections, and the
fragile exhibits, has sometimes seemed like a burden. I thought
would be much easier if the museum existed only as a virtual
presence—a book, a web site, a blog. This is kind of a "be careful
what you wish for" moment.

Q: Any perspective gained?

Yes, I'm less concerned with having the museum be taken
seriously as art, and I am just more appreciative that people are
interested in it at whatever level of involvement they choose.

Q: What happens to the museum when you are gone?

A good and as yet unresolved question. I have not yet found
anyone with the fanatical devotion required to take over someone
else's project. Most people I know have their own creative projects
that are the focus of their attention.

The physical objects in the exhibits are mostly pretty delicate,
so sale and dispersal would be a problem. The web site will
continue until some technical change renders it obsolete. The
books are in a sense a bid for limited immortality. I imagine that
if I get enough of them out there, they will circulate around, and
people will be discovering them for quite a while, like a legendary
obscure volume discovered in a dusty used-book shop.

Q: Final thoughts?

I will turn 70 this year (2020) and have no idea how much time
I have left. My father wrote his autobiography when he was 67,
formatted as a year-by-year account, illustrated with photographs,
and primarily focused on his experiences as a reconnaissance pilot

in the Second World War. He lived another 33 years after that, productive to the end.

My mother lived long as well but was debilitated by dementia and failing eyesight. My brother died of a heart attack at 51, so it seems my options are to go at any moment, decline slowly and inexorably as my mother did, or have another good three decades. Or, most likely, something totally unexpected will happen.

I am at the age where I think about death frequently and I vacillate between thinking I need to focus, get a lot done, and leave behind a worthwhile legacy, versus feeling that nothing really matters in the long run and I'll be dead anyway, just a minor blip in the space-time continuum.

HOW THE CYBERNETIC AQUARIUM CAME TO BE

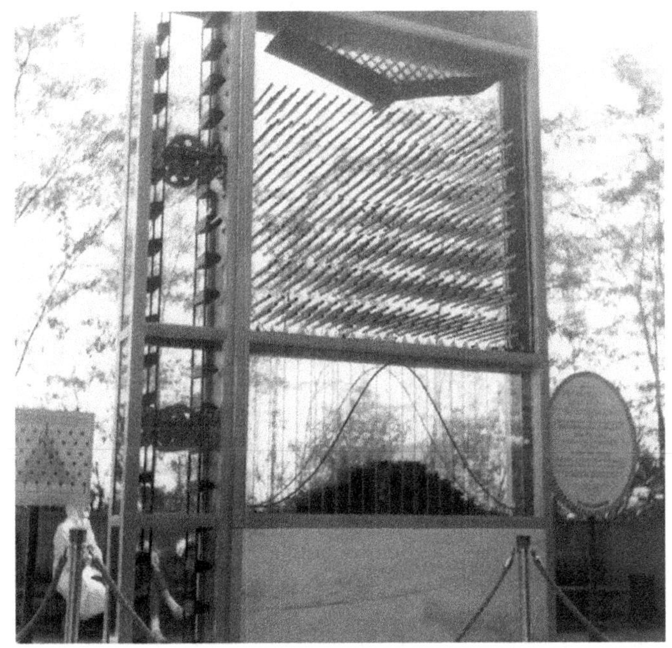

Galton board

THE WINDING ROAD

> Order in Apparent Chaos: I know of scarcely anything so apt to
> impress the imagination as the wonderful form of cosmic order
> expressed by the Law of Frequency of Error. The law would have
> been personified by the Greeks and deified, if they had known of it. It
> reigns with serenity and in complete self-effacement amidst the wildest
> confusion. The huger the mob, and the greater the apparent anarchy,
> the more perfect is its sway. It is the supreme law of Unreason.
> Whenever a large sample of chaotic elements are taken in hand and
> marshalled in the order of their magnitude, an unsuspected and most
> beautiful form of regularity proves to have been latent all along.
> —Francis Galton, Natural Inheritance (1889)

The first glimmerings of the Cybernetic Aquarium can be traced back to an exhibit at the Pacific Science Center (a remnant of the 1962 Seattle World's Fair). It was a device, known as a Galton board after its inventor, consisting of a triangular array of pegs through which a small steel balls were fed one at a time. The pegs were situated so that when a ball falls and hits a peg, it has an even chance to go left or right. Any given ball's eventual location at the bottom is random, but the resulting pile is always close to a bell-shaped curve. The more balls fed, the more certain that the final shape of the curve will match a specific curve, and that curve can be precisely defined with an equation.

To my 17-year-old mind, this was more than a mathematical demonstration. Like Galton, it seemed to me physical evidence of something profound, something going on behind the scenes, an absolute order in apparent disorder. Part of the quote above was noted on my copy of the brochure from that visit, copied from an exhibit sign.

Another seed was planted during visits to the Steinhart Aquarium in San Francisco, a wonderland of odd reptiles and amphibians, along with vast tanks of pulsing jellyfish, tentacled creatures, rooted plant-like animals, and much more. The sea was a fantastically alien world, but undeniably real. Gravity was mostly irrelevant, legs were optional, and the whole environment was filled with strange creatures, large and small. This held even down to the microscopic level, where I could see whole ecosystems in a single drop of sea water.

I loved going with my father, a college biology teacher, on field trips to the local tide pools. I never set up a true aquarium of my own, but I did enjoy capturing pollywogs and watching them grow legs and turn into tree frogs. They seemed to be magical beings that lived in both in both aquatic and arboreal worlds.

Fast forward to the 1970s, past the whirlwind of an urban college and the psychedelic sixties, where I am still trying to figure out a career path, with the difficulty of being interested in too many things. College simply expanded my range of interests from math, physics, and natural history to include art, literature, linguistics, sociology, and more.

I ended up getting training in an allied health field, respiratory therapy, to have a salable skill. The actual job didn't really suit me, but I learned a lot about how bodies function. I was especially taken by the various mechanisms that bodies have to maintain equilibrium through a complex set of sensors and feedback loops.

The computer era begins

When I was in college, computers were unwieldy beasts, requiring laborious punch card inputs and reams of paper output for even the simplest task. Once computers evolved keyboard inputs and graphics capability, I found them much more compelling. They became much more accessible and prevalent while I was working in hospitals.

I taught myself programming and quickly became my department's computer guy. Self-instruction in coding works well because of its mix of logic and experiment. For any particular concept, you can test it out, experiment, and learn what works and what doesn't, getting an immediate success-or-failure response. Another feedback loop.

There was something profoundly appealing to me about creating something, especially a something that does something, from abstract concepts such as algorithms, mathematical relations, and the grammar and structure of a programming language. I saw programming as being much like an sorcerer's incantation–if you get the words exactly, something magical happens. Unlike prayer, the result is guaranteed; it's not a request to be granted, denied, or ignored.

In the 1980s, I finally settled on a career. I got a master's degree in Medical Information Science, specializing in data visualization. Programming , my new salable skill, , was much more suitable to me as an introvert and idea-oriented person. It had interesting content (how human perception affects the translation of raw data into useful knowledge), and some creativity (visual design of data sets).

I knew from my work with intensive care monitoring data which variables were useful in diagnosis and treatment decisions, and how their complex interrelationships worked mathematically. My graduate project was to create a computer program to visualize these relationships and show that that visualization would help make accurate diagnosis and successful treatment more likely.

I worked at the university as a programmer for research projects. I liked being able to work in an academic environment without actually being an academic, as that would require specialization. I continued the theme of being between definitions, working as a software engineer with a liberal arts degree and being an artist with no formal training (but too knowledgeable to be considered an outsider artist).

Whole systems

As a young amateur naturalist I had always been more interested in ecology than taxonomy, Identifying plants and animals using field guides to identify flowers, birds, mushrooms, and so forth was less interesting to me than how these creatures lived their lives and especially how the complex web of relationships worked, and, again, the feedback loops in nature. Predators consume prey, for example, but the prey evolves defense, and the predator evolves in response.

In the 1970s, I had subscribed to CoEvolution Quarterly (later the Whole Earth Review), fascinated by their systems approach.

In graduate school I took a course in systems theory, basically a way to think of medical issues as part of a whole system.

Around this time (the 1980s), there was lots of buzz about a number of promising new ways of looking at things, generally under the heading of "complexity." These ideas included emergent properties, chaos theory, generative systems, and artificial life.

Emergent phenomena are similar in particle physics to Galton's notion of order arising from disorder. For example, a gas consists of a vast number of individual particles moving essentially at random, bouncing off each other. Taken as a whole, however, a gas has measurable qualities (pressure, volume, and temperature, each in precise mathematical relationship to the others) that are not predictable from the properties of the individual particles.

Chaos is an anarchic counterpoint to Galton's divine order in randomness. It showed that in some cases an outcome of a process or even a mathematical formula was unpredictable even if all the initial conditions are known precisely.

Generative systems are a way of actively creating organized systems that prevail against entropy, which is the inexorable tendency of systems to run down from an orderly state to a disorderly one. Relatively simple sets of rules, if carefully selected, can create organized systems. Examples are grammar in language, creating meaning by organizing basic vocabulary, or the instruction set contained in DNA for creating a living being. One experiment around this time was a demonstration that bird flocking could be simulated by having each simulated bird follow a few local rules.

I was especially taken with the idea of artificial life. This was computer simulation of various processes that are similar to biology. I created a first version of the "Virtual Aquarium" on one of the earliest Apple Macintoshes.

Silicon Valley and beyond

Eventually jobs in academia faded away and I ended up in the new boom "town" of Silicon Valley (which was more of a lifestyle and mindset than a specific location). I landed a cushy 9-to-5(ish) programming job at Sun Microsystems that was sufficiently interesting. Although the work was unrelated to medicine or science, I enjoyed designing user interfaces and visualizing data.

However, I did not want to be doing recreational programming in my spare time. Instead, my weekends were spent putting together decayed and natural found objects into surreal assemblages and dioramas, which evolved into the Zymoglyphic Museum.

My idealism about data visualization became clouded over with time. I had thought that people would make better decisions if they had access to a better understanding of the data, but it turned out most people just wanted some way of showing data that supported their pre-conceived ideas. This was true in academia and especially so in a corporate context.

Skipping ahead a few decades: I retired from Silicon Valley and moved to Portland, Oregon, and set up a new, improved, much larger version of the museum. The idea of a virtual aquarium was still percolating in my brain. Personal computer technology had progressed enough that it was relatively easy to create animations. Spending quality time on the computer was a nice way for a lifelong Californian to adapt to long rainy Oregon winters!

I revisited the fields that had seemed so promising in the 1980s and 90s. They had now had some three decades to prove their worth, but really very little had come of them. Fractals (intricate self-referential mathematical objects) had become very useful in creating naturalistic detail and other special effects in Hollywood movies. Artificial intelligence (basically non-statistical pattern recognition) is becoming more and more the basis of much of how people interact with the computerized world, but that is not an area of interest for me.

In general, complexity-related fields and the whole systems approach did not dislodge the standard reductionist approach in scientific research, which continued its successes. Artificial life, in particular, had petered out as a research field.

Still, the ideas resonated with me. As with the museum, it made sense to think of an artificial life as an art project rather than truly scientific research. That allows me to synthesize ideas from widely disparate fields of inquiry and maybe even come up with something new.

THE AQUARIUM

Not a movie, not a video game

My original vision for this project was to create a "living painting," a flat object that would hang on your wall, its contents being created as you view it. Unlike a movie, it would never repeat. Like a painting, there would be little to no user interaction, just contemplation combined with whatever the viewer's inner response might be.

Under the hood, this project would be an opportunity to explore a number of themes, such as order and disorder, how the complexity of life arises from basic principles, emergent behavior, and of course probability and feedback loops. These ideas would not necessarily be something apparent to the viewer.

My external goal, at least in retrospect, was to create a compelling artwork that extended the themes of the museum as an exhibit that people could enjoy without necessarily understanding the underlying ideas. My internal goal was to create art using basic principles that underlie the workings of nature and express them in a creative way.

Why an aquarium?

A standard domestic aquarium is already a sort of living sculpture, outwardly prosaic and serene, but inwardly encapsulating an alien world with endlessly strange aquatic life that lives by different rules. It's something you look at, maybe ponder, but it's not very interactive. This fit the design criterion of ever-changing view, but requiring little to no interaction.

The fascination of an aquarium lies in the alien nature of the aquatic environment, especially in the sea. Since the influence of gravity is minimal, the field of view can be filled with creatures from top to bottom. All size ranges exist from massive to microscopic. Creatures pulsate, dart, consume each other, drift lazily by, sway, and so forth. Gravity is only a minor consideration here, plant life is rare, and animals can look like plants, rocks, or even blobs.

The Cybernetic Universe

A computer is a good medium for this sort of project. Individual organisms can be represented internally as units of programming code, each with its own genome of properties (e.g., color), variables (current location), and behavioral instructions, such as defining a method for calculating its next move. These functions can simulate the randomness, noise, and feedback loops that are needed to test the hypothesis that feedback loops can create unplanned structure out of randomness.

There are a number of notable differences between the physical and cybernetic universes. In the latter, a world such as the aquarium is clearly a product of intelligent design by a specific creator. A biological creature's genetic code is the notoriously convoluted result of millions of years of continuous evolution, but a programming project can begin with a blank slate.

In addition to a creator, a cybernetic world assumes a viewer. Its creatures have no need to eat, excrete, reproduce, age, or die. They can be programmed to simulate those things, but basically their only survival requirement is to be interesting. This requirement necessitates, at a minimum, a visible appearance of some kind, some motion and/or growth, and interaction with others.

Design goals

One approach to creating an aquarium in a computer would be to make it as lifelike as possible, with realistic fish swimming in plausible motions. This seems to me as pointless as a photorealistic drawing; there needs to be some creative component in addition to the representational, some component that is unique to the medium that is used. I wanted this aquarium to be rather an ecosystem of creatures native to the cybernetic universe, simple abstractions with lifelike qualities.

Exploring new algorithms and creating tiny abstract animalcules that do unpredictable things has a mad scientist/alchemist appeal but the result is not necessarily art. Many experiments in artificial life illustrate similar algorithmic content, but they have little visual appeal. For this project, I wanted to give consideration to composition and symbolic content.

A computer-specific goal in actually building the project was to make the code as simple and well-organized as possible. Simple is easier to maintain than complex, but beyond the practicality there is a secret satisfaction in elegant code; secret because it's entirely possible no one else will ever see it. The internal structure of the code corresponds to the creatures on the screen. Not having interactivity in the design helps to make this easier.

THE ECOSYSTEM

The actual creation of the aquarium proceeded along my usual lines of trial and error. I experimented with algorithms and feedback loops to see if I could make cybernetic creatures that had lifelike properties.

Social circles

It was once believed that if you knew the position and velocity of every particle in the universe, you could in theory predict the future. That turns out not to be true even in some surprisingly simple cases. If two celestial bodies orbit each other, such as the earth and moon, it's possible to predict their motions so precisely that eclipses can be predicted to minute many years in advance. However, three or more bodies of approximately equal size, orbiting each other, become a chaotic system whose path is difficult or impossible to predict even if you know the precise location and velocity of those bodies.

This "three-body problem" inspired a simple algorithm for

creature interaction: each one simply follows the closest neighbor that is not the one headed toward the creature. A "creature" in this case is simply a colored circle. With each iteration, a circle follows another which in turn follows another. The result is a stately, hypnotic dance that never comes to a stop or settles into a repeating pattern. Creatures form little groups and trains, which break up as each one finds another one to follow. I have no idea if this algorithm is innovative or obvious, but it suited my purpose - a simple feedback loop that creates a complex, unpredictable, appealing output. I called this algorithm "social circles."

Dots and lines

My next experiment was to see if I could make something lifelike using just the most primitive graphic elements (circles and lines) and basic motion type (predictable and random). The simplest motion that keeps a particle visible on the screen is a particle that moves in a straight line and bounces off the edge of the screen like a billiard ball, the epitome of predictable motion. I added oscillation (another predictable motion) to the otherwise dull little lines so that their tails would sway like tiny metronomes as they moved.

To complement the lines, I created some little circles (dots) that move about randomly. Each dot moves in a random direction for a random distance, so any given move is not predictable. This algorithm simulates the motion that results when microscopic particles are constantly jostled by the thermal jitter of surrounding molecules.

Primordial Soup

The dots and lines were programmed so that they would hook together if their respective motions brought them into close proximity. These compound organisms embodied randomness, linearity, and rhythm. The results actually did seem lifelike. It struck me as a symbolic re-enactment of the origin of life, connecting simple molecules into complex ones.

In a representational painting, such as a landscape, there is

often a "witness," a human or other conscious observer, to serve
as a proxy for the viewer. Some of the animated molecules were
headed up by an "eye," a dark circle within a lighter one that
moved toward the closest creature. This simple action makes the
creature not only seem alive, but conscious on some level.

Jellyfish always represented to me some quintessence of aquatic
serenity; they just pulse and float about. I added colored circles to
the soup that used the "social circles" algorithm for their motion,
along with a simple pulsing internal rhythm. These "pulsoids"
provide a tranquil counterpoint to the lively dance of the
animated molecules.

Now that I had the (very) basic design for my creatures, I
needed an aquarium for them to be in. I added backgrounds and
foregrounds to it to give a (non-literal) sense of being underwater,
and, just as a biological aquarium owner might decorate their
tanks with little castles, pirate chests, driftwood, and plastic plants.

Microbiota

I decided to create a second aquarium tank from scratch rather
than keep adding new species to the original one. Primordial
Soup was inspired by principles from physical laws and the origin
of life from those principles. The second aquarium, Microbiota,
was inspired by biological processes. Instead of thinking in terms
of atoms and molecules, I imagined simple creatures that could
grow and reproduce.

These new creatures are essentially an evolution of the pulsoids
from Primordial Soup. These new versions grow limbs, which
are purely ornamental and not used in locomotion. Instead of
the loose and self-assembling line segments of Primordial Soup,
limbs are lines that sprout from a creature's core. Each line
grows to a pre-determined length, spawns another, and sways
at a predetermined rate. The animated molecules in Primordial
Soup assembled themselves; there was no central organization. In
more complex creatures there is internal coordination, in biology
known as morphogenesis.

The pulsoids in Primordial Soup were distinguished from each

other by their randomly assigned colors and sizes. The addition
of the limbs, each with its own distinctive motion, gave each of
the new creatures its own individual personality.

In Primordial Soup, creatures die if they fall off the screen
and are replaced by clones. In microbiota, the same rule applies
except that all creatures have a primitive genome that gets passed
to its replacement. The genome consists simply of a list of traits
such as number of limbs or the maximum length of its limb
segments. Each trait is randomized before the handoff. This
results in a population with a wide variety of appearances and
motions and thus personalities.

Since there is no evolutionary pressure in this world, no
competition for resources as is found in nature, all varieties are
equally well adapted for survival. This is similar to the time in
Earth's history before predators evolved.

A museum exhibit

I wasn't sure at first whether a computer project could be part of
the Zymoglyphic Museum, or if it would just stand on its own. At
first glance it does not seem to fit with the theme of the aesthetics
of decay. The museum's organic exhibits are a paean to entropy:
rusty metal, the arrested decay of taxidermy, a celebration
of bringers of disorder such as cobwebs and fungi, not shiny
electronics.

The aquarium motif actually fits well with Zymoglyphic
history. One of my first museum creations, even before the
museum itself existed, was a large dehydrated aquarium/
diorama, something that might have been found in a parlor
during the Age of Wonder. That led to a series of little dioramas
using 10-gallon aquarium tanks as a frame.

The cybernetic version of the aquarium also fit in the Modern
Age wing of the museum as an example of an innovative medium
for continuing the exploration of perennial themes, such as order
and disorder, and the search for novel representations of the
primordial ooze.

This project also continues the theme of "happy accidents"

that can result from an intuitive approach to art. Trying to create a sort of spontaneous combustion by mixing algorithms is analogous to collage and assemblage, an intuitive arrangement of existing things to creates something new and surprising.

FUTURE EVOLUTION

My fantasy as a creator would be to create a little world that would run on its own, given a few starting points, with results both unexpected and delightful. It would be nice to be able to rely on such semi-magical concepts such as self-assembly and emergent properties to create interesting and novel aquarium inhabitants. The reality is that, unless the initial conditions are carefully chosen, most such creations will be too fast or too slow, crowded or overly sparse, or otherwise just unwatchable.

One way out of this is to apply, as nature does, the biological principle of natural selection. Creatures could be automatically selected for their desirability and they already have primitive genomes that could be expanded. However, implementing "natural selection" requires some sort of selection criteria. In the physical world, the basic criterion is physical survival, being able to access sunlight, water, nutrients, and mates in competition with others seeking same. In the virtual world, that criterion would be the survival of the most interesting, and that is something which cannot be defined in a way that creates unexpected outcomes.

The final challenge of the aquarium has been writing about it. The exhibit itself, billed as "The Aquarium of Tomorrow," has been popular in the museum as a hypnotic, if simple, display. None of the underlying ideas that I found so inspiring are evident to the viewer, so I'm experimenting with various ways of making them more accessible, to lay bare its inner workings.

Writing is itself a way of continuing the theme of creating order from the chaos of ideas that swarm in my head, much as digital plankton, made of basic alphabet particles, the fragments sometimes linear, sometimes random, come alive when they connect in just the right way.

Portrait Gallery

James Gouldthorpe

James Gouldthorpe is an artist and photographer who visited the museum's Bay Area incarnation in 2013. You can see more of his work at jgouldthorpe.com

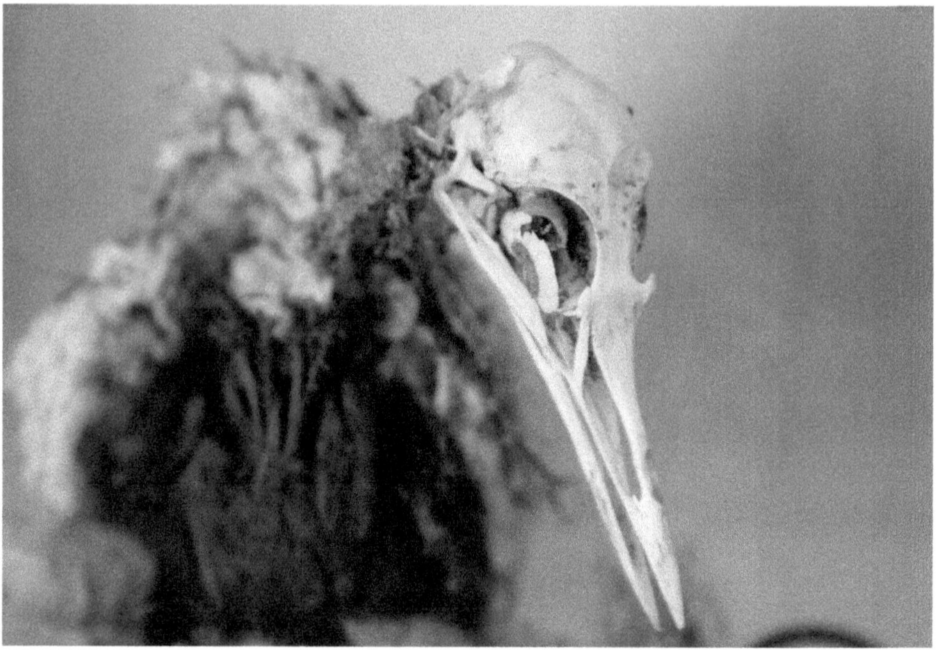

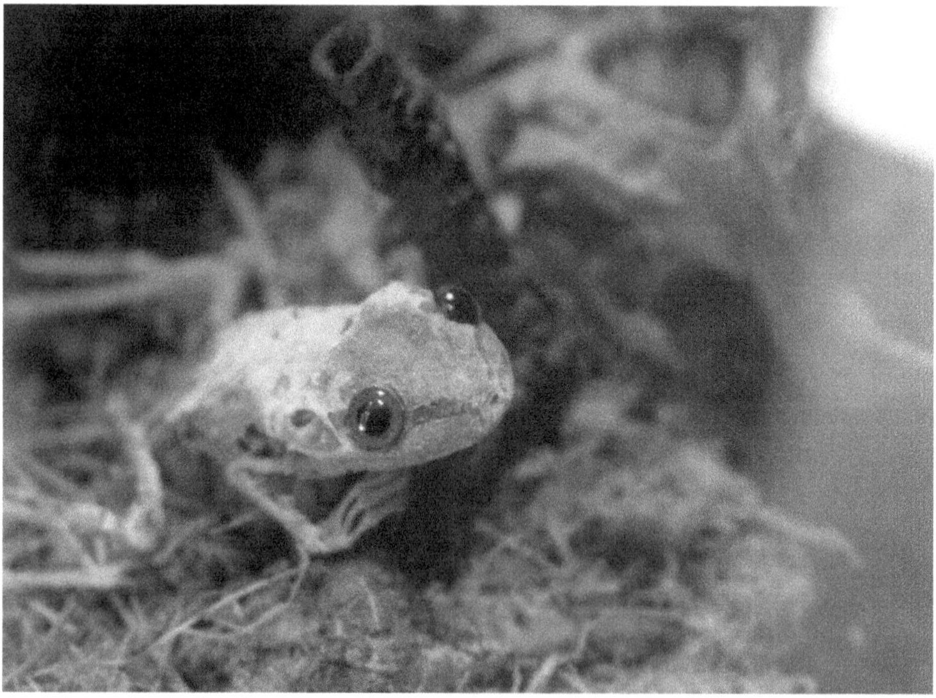

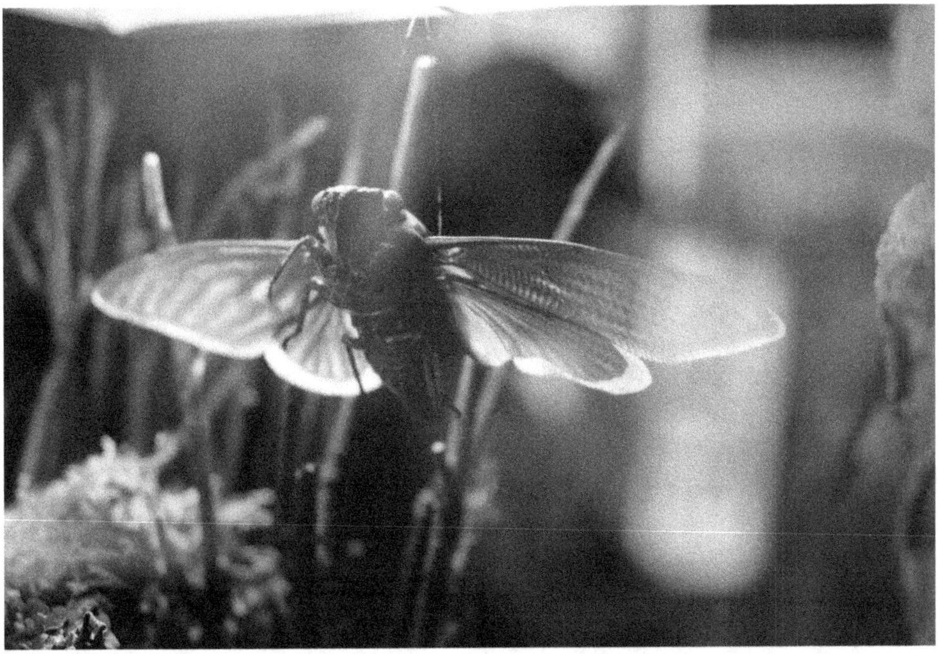

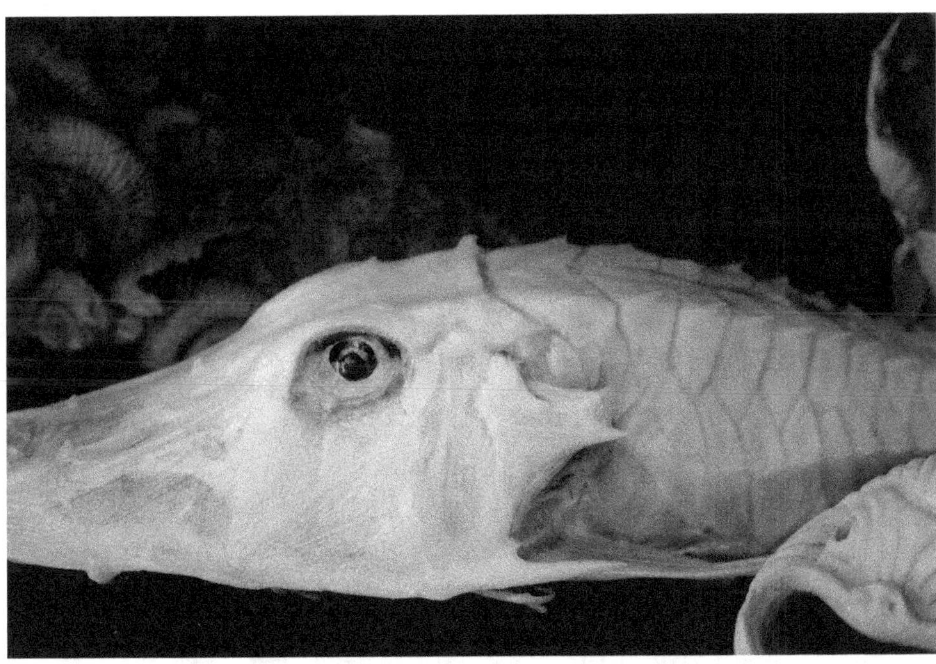

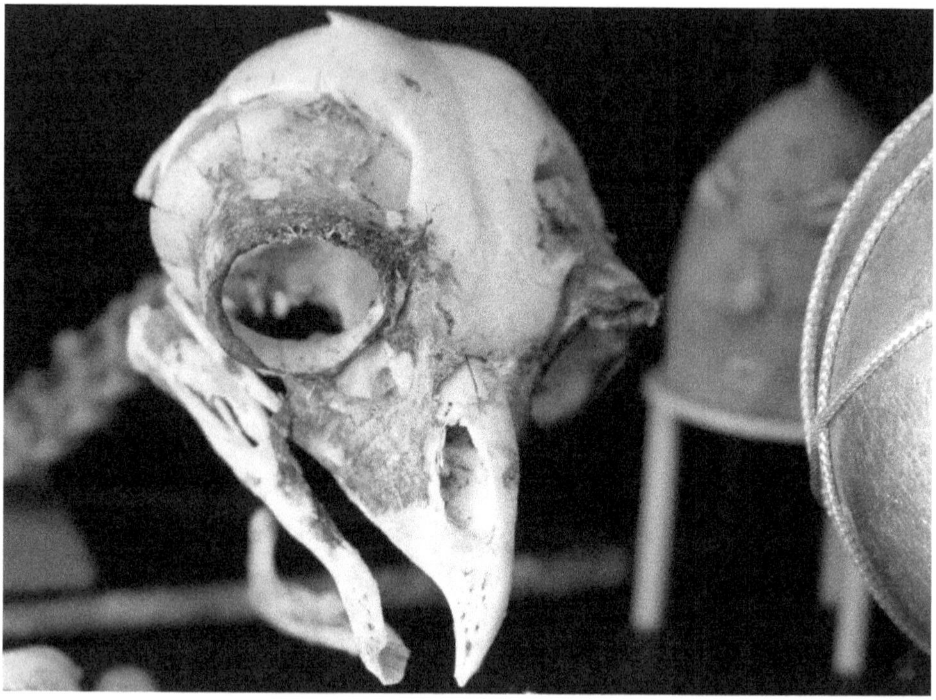

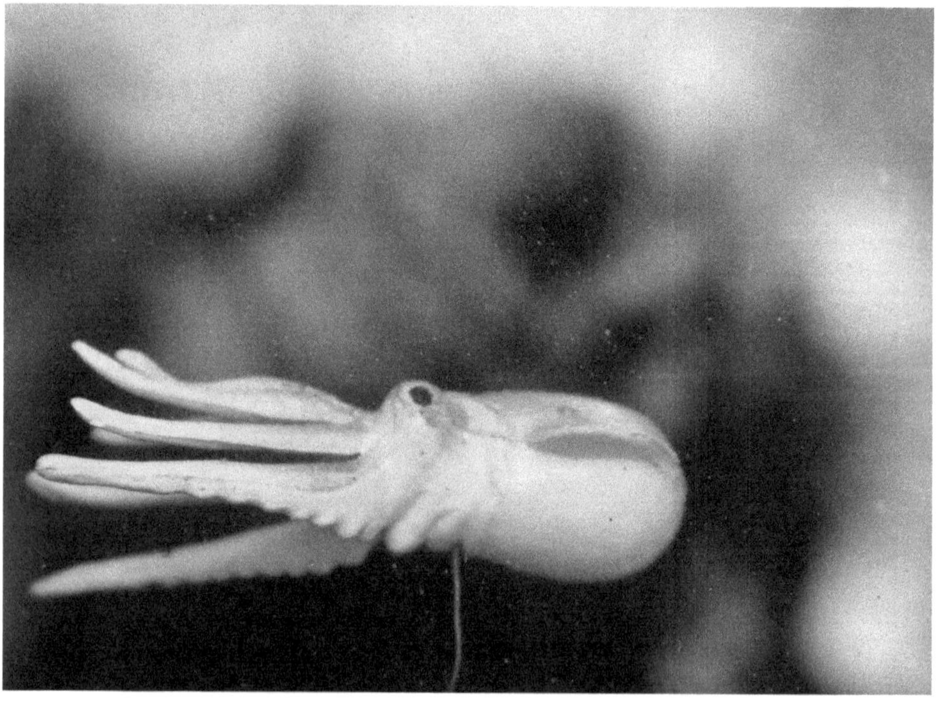

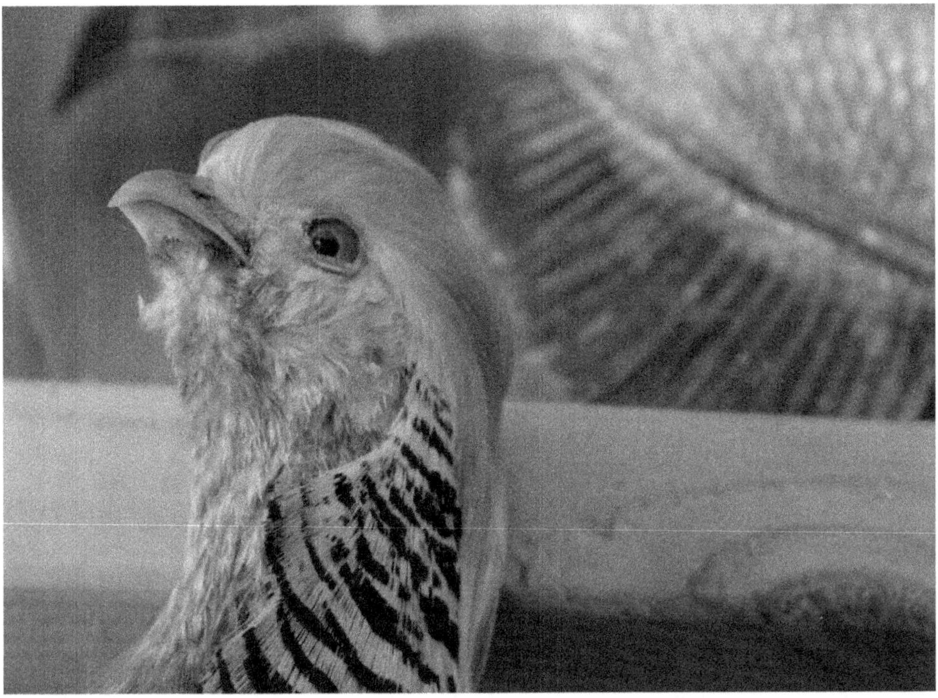

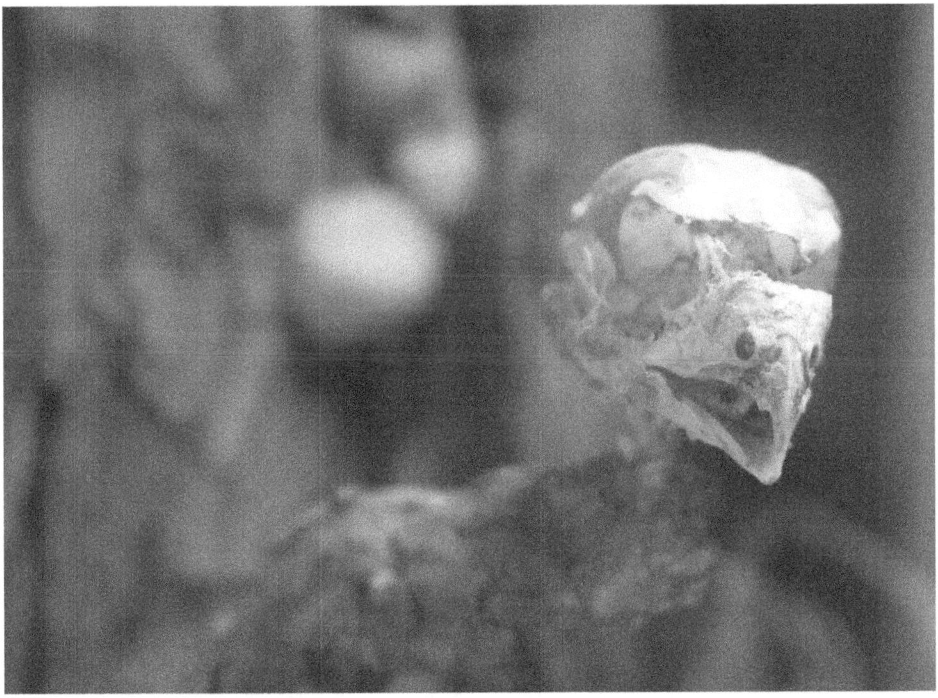

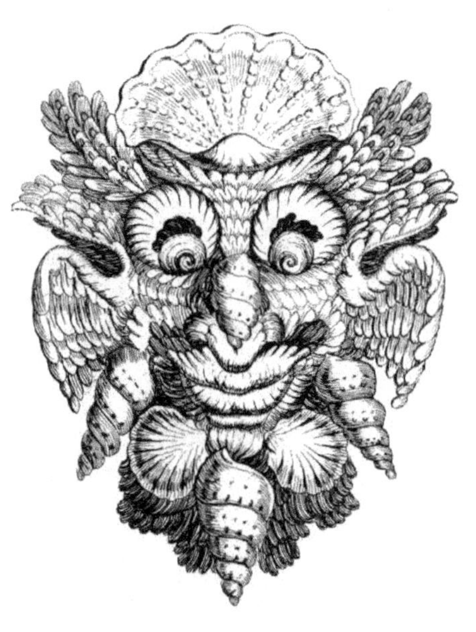

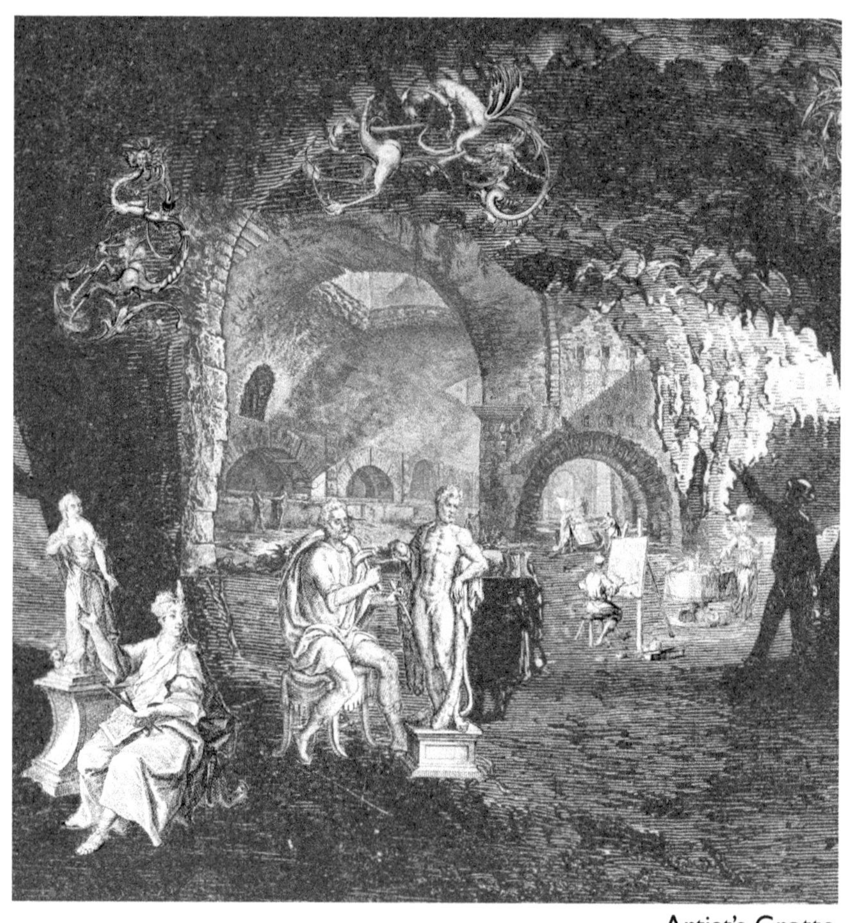

Artist's Grotto

2. THE CREATIVE COMMUNITY

IN MY DREAM...

Jason Squamata

Jason Squamata is a writer and spoken-word artiste. He was a contributor to the first *Zymoglyphic Anthology* and is the author of *Hotel Zymoglyphic* (The Zymoglyphic Museum Press, 2019) and *Hypnozine* (Deep Overstock, 2020).

The following pieces are from *Oneiric Memoir: The Dream Diaries of Jason Squamata* (The Zymoglyphic Museum Press, 2020).

His work may be found at patreon.com/squamata, including spoken word interpretations of his writings.

Dreams have always been fundamental to my creative process and my experience of reality (such as it is), but I've been trepidatious about presenting these by-products of my Orakuloid practice as "entertainment."

The symbolic codes and gestures and presences that cohere in the dreaming space are so personal.

...

Miraculous mutations reported on with piercing precision and occasional infestations of trans-oneiric irony. And that desolate wind of longing that blows always between the many worlds.

...

Remember as you read and as your own life is read that it's from the depths that tomorrow comes. Look not to the skies for meaning or salvation but into the abyss of your own unbeing.

...

Marry the emblems and eidolons and eerie icons you smuggled back to the unfolding structures and oracular rhythms of your awakening intelligence.

...

Collect the spectral slivers of the mirror you break by looking too deeply. A list of throbbing details. Micromoments of virile, viral fictoplasm.

The magick words that invoke this Orakulism in its purest state?

"In my dream..."

—Jason Squamata

from the introduction to *Oneiric Memoir*

*In my dream, I decide that my function in the scheme of things is
to do nothing but dream.*

Nothing but dreaming and dictation.

When I just can't sleep, I can study the nature of the dreaming
faculty itself and watch my own mind's music get rich and
prismatic as I consume all these mirrors with my fractalizing
palace of memory.

There's a montage of strange equipment getting gassed up,

like every apparently random image and object in this room

is a component in an astral engine

that digests dreamjizz and thereby generates a murder of
fragmented brain babies,

black feathers beating and holy terror shrieked in a dungeon no
bigger than my head.

The texture mapping is so distinct when the dream ends

that opening my eyes is like peeling cellophane from my face

to see the same patch of plumbing, with just a million more pixels
of gravitas.

All the dreams are gone.

A big empty space.

I'm leading a tour of the book I'm editing.

It's a living thing, hovering and throbbing and shifting its shape, revolving a few feet above a stroboscopic dancefloor pentagram. The tour is made up of potential investors. We're all wearing wetsuits that are filigreed with fiberoptic tattoos and designed for deep immersion and interface with sentient narrative tulpa-clusters.

There's a feedback loop that comes on when you do lots of diving. I'm always embedded in some kind of narrative, wherein I usually go diving into a deeper degree of narrative and feel a strange metabolic nostalgia for the diver I was in the level above. I feel like I know what I'm doing, but I may have sketchy description and blurry details on the part of my narrator to thank for my expertise.

The storytelling instinct is, in some ways, superficial.

You don't know everything your characters know. You don't need a PhD to write a physicist. You pick the details that vibrate, the nuances that sound good and speak volumes. You fake the rest and somehow the music fills in all the blanks and the fictoplasmic beast in question accrues an intensity that competes with and maybe supplants "reality".

That's what I'm telling the investors.

It's my standard prologue.

I always say it like I'm making it up as I go.

We dive.

Into my client's book.

Into fleshscapes soaked and coated by cascading latex, into dubstepped Escherplexes and prismatic, chittering elf-holes and tattooed skinstorms that explode into perfume. My suit grows big scissors at the wrists, like garden-shears with glo-in-the-dark glyphs engraved on the blades. Faucets in my codpiece release a luminous glue. Luminous and endless. Rapture achieved and sustained.

Fragments of feeling and mis-en-scene careen towards us like rogue galaxies, enveloping us utterly, and we're lost in Her life for just a moment or a year and then my Hypnovision kicks in. The scissorbirds sing. Then the myth is in pieces. The erotics of collage. The investors get lost from time to time as we go deeper, as we enter the static time and mutable space of an artifact, a host of ghosts that hang suspended in everywhen until the reading mind catches fire and the visions kick in.

I sometimes split myself into seven people and go on a rescue binge that seems to take decades. But the key harmonic sings us home and I can hear my client's laughter like a doll does when playtime is about to begin in earnest and the dollhouse cosmos flexes, in a sense, and I see the hot pink heart of all this, of Her, of the Work, regulating the immaterial tides, here at the molten core of everything that isn't. I bask in its atomic truth. My microselves and my macroselves and who I am now are aligned. I feel the big picture in a synaptic sherbet-storm that lesser men might mistake for a seizure.

She's eaten the investors, it seems.

They will pass through Her lyrical complexity

and emerge on the other side of summer as soft serve solid gold.

I'm wandering the dusty silver surface of an astral moon, a moon of the mind.

This is where vast ideas often crash in a cabbalistic cosmos, beached on the threshold of manifestation. I'm wandering through the wreckage of a hundred stories I have started and abandoned over the decades. Some of them are wispy little ships, made of a title and some oozing ambiance and a few twisted scenes, disfigured on impact. Some of them are so dense and baroque that it's a wonder they made it this far, like fractalizing cathedral engines made of character clusters and songlines and collages of research and scorched master plots.

I have maps in my backpack, old notebooks and beat sheets and messy first draft recordings on cassette. The derelict beauty of this territory is awesome in the truest sense and vaguely terrifying.

A strange music emanates from the husks as a brittle lunar wind blows through them. I feel great shame and regret, seeing how much beauty I have failed to draw through the gate into print and publication. I feel painfully estranged from the numinous wellsprings each structure was born in. A sprawling necropolis of miscarriages. I wonder if I deserve to wake up and sustain my own manifestation when I have failed so many millions of my implicit dream children.

But I hear something suddenly that slivers the operatic gloom of it all.

Spooky swamp boogie voodoo music, a lascivious bass line slithering in pools of static abstraction. Devilish pillow talk issuing through a broken ghost radio.

I follow the slither to its source, a ramshackle death ship made of rudely grafted bits and pieces, souls and scenes and vicious little voices from my current work in progress.

Seeing it from the underside of the mind, it has more meat and life and jangling jeweled beauty than I would have expected. It's humming, rumbling, belching Pentecostal flumes of black fire and lightning.

A female version of me is deep in its viscera, supervising her greasy clones in a passionate act of reconstruction. She smiles when she sees me, says there's life in all of these monsters. They only require my voice and my absolute immersion.

An armada of dream monsters, ready to shred planet Malkuth into silver ribbons whenever I'm ready. The repairs and reboots and surgeries are ongoing, she says.

The fire is mine, she says.

I notice with a ticklish sensation that the female me is somehow beautiful.

She says I can't kiss her clones until the craft in question is in flight.

Fair enough, I say. Time to get busy. Everlastingly.

An ibis-headed hobo is standing in the doorway of a room I used to live in,

beckoning with a ceremonial gesture,

inviting me to join him on a stroll

through every space I've ever occupied,

all the rooms and streets and natural spaces I've moved through since birth, recreated perfectly

and woven together

in a chaotic museum

that pixellates in the places I can't quite remember.

I ask him why I've always felt like a stranger in my own body.

He speaks in trumpety tones that are conveniently subtitled.

"You're just passing through.

From nowhere to nowhere.

Every kiss is a silent good-bye.

You are just...

passing...

through."

Superman, the alien sun god, the almost omnipotent Buddha of compassion, dresses up like a frumpy schlub and goes to work, presumably so he doesn't turn into an asshole.

However cosmic your private life might seem, however strange and intense your performances might get, however deep and rich and mysterious your evenings of voodoo scribbling might be, there's always an office where Perry White will remind you of the Daily Planet's expectations and the little ways in which you fail to meet them.

You learn to stare at his coffee and subtly sublimate it with your laser vision, secretly letting off a little steam so you don't go Bizarro and set the city on fire.

You're thankful for surveillance and mandatory etiquettes because these moments test your commitment to your cover identity.

Thank you, Mr. White.

I'll try to do better.

I'll keep my feet on the ground.

I'll keep reaching for the stars.

The Voice

Listening to the inner voice at all costs is a tricky business. It often contradicts itself or says three antithetical things at the same time. It feels like destiny when the world agrees with it. When the world doesn't get it, it feels like a siren song leading you off the cliff of culture to fall from any quantifiable grace and kiss the jagged rocks of homeless lunacy.

Reason will count the times the Voice seemingly led you into ruin. The Voice will insist that trepidation has been your only sin, and you didn't throw yourself off the edge with enough force to grow wings. Your indifference to scorn or adulation means you'll make decisions based on the needs of an immaterial ecology while your body just wants you to get a job and be normal. The body wants boring things, but it wants mainly to survive. The Voice is so sure of itself that it burns up the bodies it uses, confident that another doomed dreamer will pick up the tune and be its vessel. The Voice tells you that the world should pay your meager monkish bills so these mythologies can unfold in you and on the page all day every day with no fucks given unto commerce or common comprehension. The Voice says the world needs these stories and I exist to deliver them in the manner that best suits their exotic energies.

Reason says the world will never know what it needs, more stories just thicken and confuse the soup of chaos we call a culture, and work that is written according to an inner visionary trajectory rather than according to the dubious demands and expectations of an increasingly imaginary marketplace will lead you always to the lonely room of Henry Darger or the pornopathic bughouse of the Marquis de Sade. Fortunately, time and nature and the deeply corrupt world of "reason" have taken away almost everything that mattered to me.

Even my most aspirational speculations anticipate at best a more immersive involution. With winged feet firmly planted on a vision board built to surf the vicissitudes, I hear a world of good advice behind me and before me only void and the Voice. Only the Voice and its curious emergent structures and the Tulpa clusters that grow in its flow. It says the need for a prayer to be answered or even heard makes the joyful sound within a form of extortion. I thank it for giving me no choice. It knows I can dither at the crossroads for a million years. Needing me to sit still and learn the dangers of devotion, the Voice got me pregnant with an Omniverse. Anticipating what kind of babies people pay for will not ease the pain of delivery. On the contrary. She filled me with technology. I will disconnect the discursive intellect and follow the directions, like I do every day.

If dereliction is the inevitable secret fate of every demiurge, I'll give notice before I vanish and my decay won't mess with anyone's money. But I won't withdraw from this battered avatar til these myths are written. A future generation will get it from the start. If that generation is imaginary, it's because reality didn't deserve them. And I can enjoy their understanding, because, at long last, I will be imaginary, too.

Book-writing.

Job-hunting.

Doing what I must do.

Slaving over the Parthenogenesis of The HypnoPlex and feeding slices of its time to anyone who will keep this body housed and fed long enough to weaponize my madness and complete the fundamental mission.

Make your own inner Voice be loud and clear and conscious. The Psychopompic hyperlogos is a very specialized frequency, and it's my everything. But it will leave you alone like you've never been alone and the palaces it builds are made of echoes. So it's all there is for me, but I wouldn't recommend it.

Excelsior.

—Jason Squamata, 7/4/2020

Selections from the Work

Coleman Stevenson

Coleman Stevenson is a Portland-based writer, text/image artist, and educator. She employs ritual, alchemy, and mythic archetype to fuel creative projects.

The works here are selected from the poetry collections *The accidental rarefication of pattern #5609* (Bedouin Books, 2012) and *Light Sleeper* (Deep Overstock, 2020), as well as *Color Studies of the Zymoglyphic Region* and *Meditations on the Alchemical Journey.*

See the full range of her work at colemanstevenson.com

The taxidermist

Pearl-ash.

Arsenical soap.

Corrosive sublimate.

      Do you know how to get blood out of feathers?

Press the eyes in but do not break them;

break the little bones between the orbits and the mouth.

Hoard. What you think you lack.

As a body retains water.

Be careful how you re-form the shell

once the fat is scraped away.

It can be either perched or poised for flight

but only one, then that forever.

Here in the cracked house people come and go

      more or less like anywhere else

      but when something breaks it is often in slow motion.

      We rewind, the chips and slivers recollecting

      pulling into place to make of all things: a teacup,

      and almost exactly the same one as before.

      We are pleasantly surprised when the amber wave

      sucks up into the shape of hot tea.

      We also know the opposite is true:

      a film of decomposition sped forward

      appears to reanimate a dead thing —

      the body of the little fox frantic with ants,

      the saprobic swell of hydrogen and nitrogen,

      that nods the head and wags the tail again.

      This is a semi-permanent method that does not require glue or wire.

But consider also a third option:

it is the animatronic pigeon's lack of a past that makes him perfect.

With only the pure drive to move as intended

and having nothing he knows of to lose,

he whistles open his wings, mechanizes into the rafters.

Such a beautiful sound from under the mandible.

The animatronic pigeon is chewing his ambition into a whir and buzz,

singing for his supper of nuts and bolts.

from *The accidental rarefication of pattern #5609*

The White Phase

Bowls of sawdust and tufts of feathers—

dark peel of fruit and webbed wings of bats—

the man who burns bones brushes them into

a box but can he get every speck?

Soft but dense, the smoky must of age

is chalk on my tongue in this tannic bitter tea—

hard to swallow being left behind

but I would be scattered nowhere—

I would be glass made from sand

sintered in the furnace flames.

It happens in the body, happens in the brain—

memories break to chemicals in the end

resubmitting to ether for the start-again.

In that grave, a body treated with lime

when burning to life in the cores of stars

gives off a blue-white light when it heats

as elements must have long ago

from The accidental rarefication of pattern #5609

In the world of sea monkeys, each undulation makes a wave.

Do not peek at caterpillars returned

in pupae to primordial ooze

or you will ruin the angels.

Let earthworms hacked regenerate

in damp and dark of peat—

things *want* to live.

Ferns catapult their spores

into an afternoon's hot haze

and hope to flare an army of

green arrows across the dirt.

I watch bits of lace frill and grow

inside this glass on my desk

and know I have seen the true face

of *the small*, magnified and natural

with appetite. Everything minute moves

swiftly to its orchestrated place,

a fitting form to realize every goal.

I think of beds in rooms, tightly made

and how I am made and unmade much like those

as others lie down in me and change my shape.

from *Light Sleeper*

FERMENTATION

Planetary ruler: Venus

The product of Conjunction is allowed to decay. In this period of rumination, putrefaction is considered to be a provider of new life into the Process. Symbolically, this is a pouring forth of new imagination and ideas about the self on the way towards enlightenment.

Every seed must gestate in the proper soil before it can germinate. That soil is made from a thousand dead things—husks of insects, bones ground down to dust, carcasses of leaves. From the rotten heat, a swelling, a cascade of green above and pale root below. So it is with any sort of womb, even the one your precarious heart of hearts sits in now, waiting to be measured.

from *Meditations on the Alchemical Journey*

all air and static
almost not ever there
a charge of electric blue
a thread to tie a cloud
to the ground

(School of Ephemeral Abstraction)

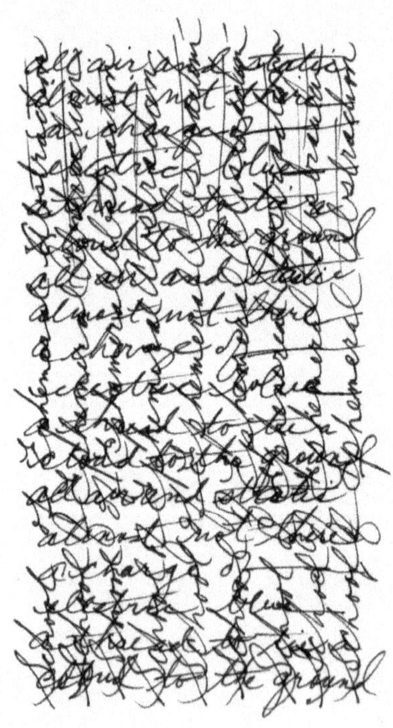

Your beloved dead
go wherever you go
riding on your back
or buried within

Your own future death
travels with you
as well, waiting for
its turn —

(Age of Wonder: Wandering
                    Burial Urn)

Writing and making art is definitely alchemy to me. It is magic. You take base elements (ideas and materials) and combine them, treat them to certain conditions, and if you do each step "properly," a whole new thing is formed. In the process, the self is transformed as well. Sometimes you don't even know how you got to gold, so it might seem like it was there all along. No. The act of doing the work, of practicing, every single time leads you to a place that is more channeled and automatic. It is a collaboration of a sort – between the self now, all the selves you've ever been, and all the ideas put into the world before you by everyone else. The more you invest in the process, the more you can become the Magician, the Alchemist.

from "Fairy Tales w/ Coleman Stevenson and Ariel Kusby" *Deep Overstock* Issue 2, June 7, 2018

PROTOTYPES

Christopher Corbell

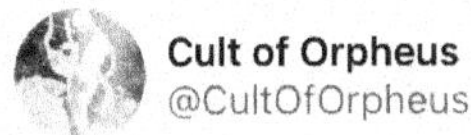

Christopher Corbell is a musician, composer and software developer. These pieces are works in progress from a forthcoming opera.

Christopher's musical work can be seen at cultoforpheus.org and his generative art software at mathaesthetics.com

Seven

From the present node there are a limited number of edges.
Seven, given no a priori restrictions.
Fewer, with biases and attachments.
The maximum by the two proposed models, either ten or eleven,
but that is not possible for us.
Seven, then.
Any more edges and the controller must group them, or ignore them.

Each node of presence is a pending traversal,
down one of seven edges to the next node -
but there is no actual node at which one arrives,
no tangible point adjacent to another tangible point
in the imagined line.

Nodes of presence are infinitely ephemeral.
This is the strong foundation.
All thought moves forward from this absolute transience.

One can intend to reverse a traversal, to
come back and choose an alternate edge, but we
are changed, and the available edges
have also changed - so reversal is itself
traversing a new edge, to a new node,
never actually a return.

It is not quite right to claim that there
is structure to the graph - it is at best
an algebra, a set of possibilities inherent
in available maneuvers, because traversal

changes the graph. Does it not create the graph?

Does the will to traverse, to escape from
the present node, emanate the graph,
consciousness like the web-spinning spider
projecting the universe of options it requires
at each instant?

If we imagine edges beyond the ones we can perceive,
a hundred or a million nodes away,
does it increase the possibility that they exist,
that we can move toward them?

A narrative recounts one traversal imperfectly,
ignoring interstitial nodes, furtive sidetracks,
retrograde loops, fuzzy states.
There were always more forms of presence, unnoticed or denied,
and imagination can create and substitute fictional nodes,
simplifications or inventions for the ones it forgets.

All narratives accumulate error.
The magnitude of the error increases faster
with belief in the narrative.
All narrative is fiction.
Therefore, internal narrative is fiction.

From the present node there are seven edges.
One may embrace an unspoken, amorphous imperative
something like this statement:
stay awake to the available edges,
hold the work of choice in reverence,

bring into each pivot, each traversal,

that which you wish to become,

that which you wish the graph, the cosmos,

to become

from your vanishing viewpoint.

Claim:

this is the responsibility of consciousness.

This is how one engages with the unmanageable complexity
encountered in the interface.

This is how one creates meaning independent of the interface.

The proof of this claim

requires incarnation.

Dissolution

Disconnected from the interface.
Maintenance boosts suspended.
My breath continues.
It sound in the hull is gentler then I expected.

Stars angle in constellations that only exist from here.
The probability is that no one else will see this.

Even at this distance
that is past all return
solitude dissolves.

This attention is the attention
of cosmos toward itself,
this metabolism legion,
even the words employed
to give form and structure to contemplation
are waveforms that have moved through other minds and tongues,
corpuscles of consciousness in the body of living language,
whisper-smuggled titan of millennia.

In saying the word 'solitude',
in feeling its grey weight upon the heart,
its peace or its abyss,
in knowing that millions of lips
have been kissed by these same three syllables
one is not alone.

Intuitive Drawings

Eileen McGarvey

Eileen McGarvey is a Portland-based artist working with fabric, dolls, and spontaneous drawing. She uses art as an emotional healing modality.

You can follow her work at instagram.com/e_mcgarvey

Intuitive Drawing Process

I have always been interested in "systems" that take some control away from the artist, access the subconscious and contribute input in some way to the final artwork. While this type of drawing practice did not originate with me, having been explored by many other artists past and present, I have my particular take on it and use it every day as a form of creative self care and contemplative practice.

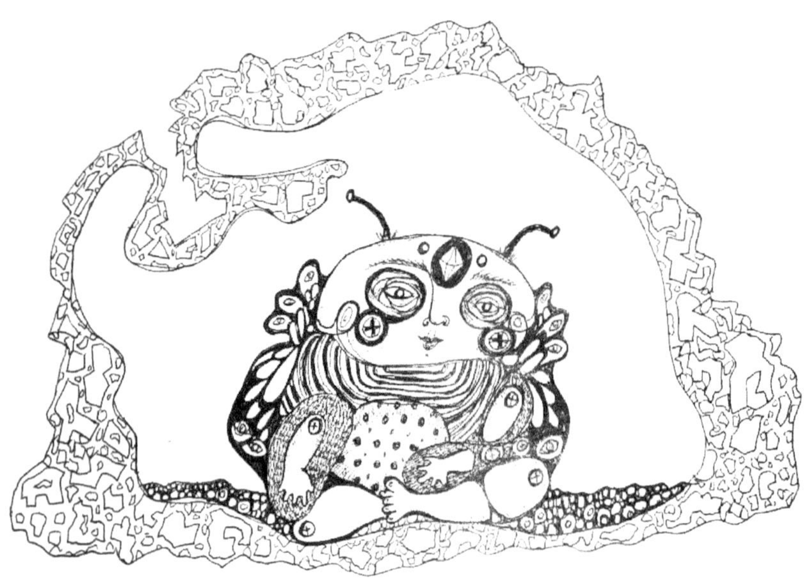

Bumble bee waiting for my wings to dry (2021)

Ingredients:

Any paper, any size - I usually use standard copy paper because it is readily available

Office pens - my favorite is a medium tip, smeary pen with dense black ink - Zebra Z-grip Flight, but I'll use anything

At least 15 minutes of undisturbed time in an undisturbable place (at work this consists of locking myself in a room for my break)

Music or white noise to drown out extraneous sound.

Recipe:

Put the conscious, thinking part of the brain in the back seat until needed later when you are reflecting and interpreting.

Clear your mind, breathe and feel into your body.

Let your hand and body transmit through the pen and across the paper in any speed, direction or mark-making that feels "right". Give yourself over to process. You can do it with eyes open or shut. My line is usually continuous

Continue until you feel done and have enough "material" to work with.

Turn the paper in all directions and let your conscious mind gently try to "read" and interpret the lines. Sometimes it will come right away and I draw from start to finish, other times I just go to an area that intrigues me and start to experiment with it, adding line, shape, texture or pattern. Accentuating some lines, connecting what seems like it needs to be connected. Continuing lines that feel like they need to be continued. Without judgment, note any emotion or feeling of needing to control outcome, and let this go.

If words or phrases arise strongly in your mind, write or draw them. I usually include them as part of the drawing and they sometimes start to inform the drawing, other times they are seemingly unrelated. Continue on this way letting the conscious and subconscious take turns giving you direction.

Work with the drawing until it feels finished. I usually put the date and a title if one comes to me.

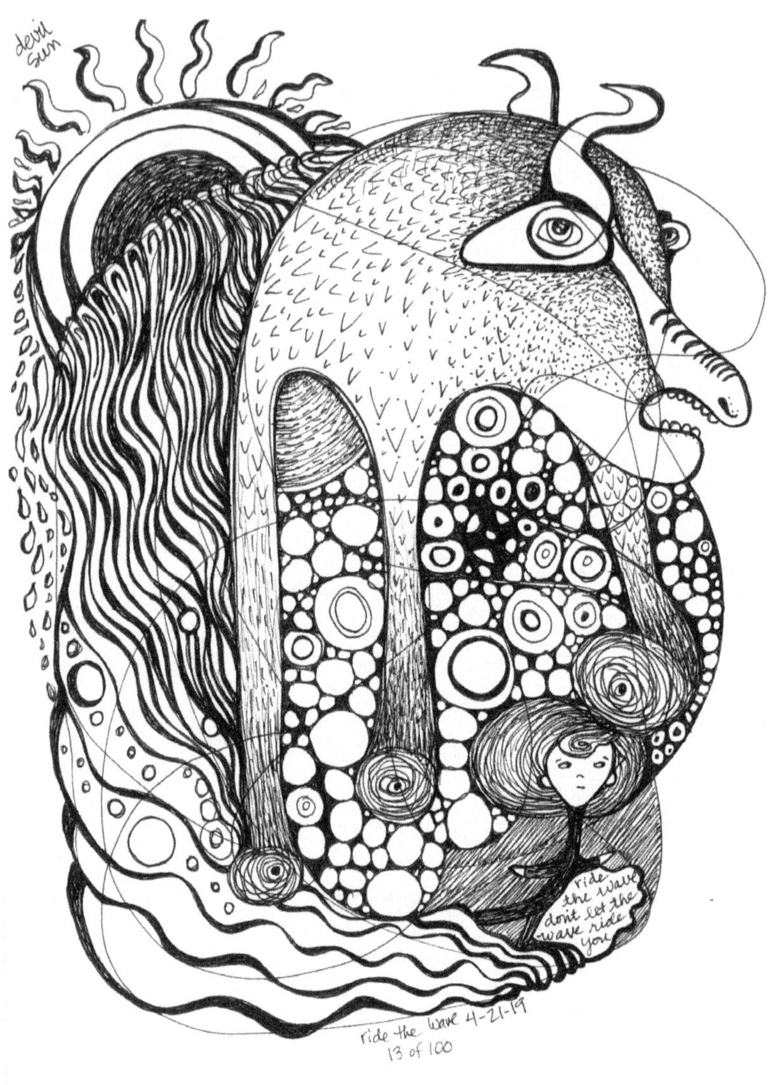

Ride the wave (2019)

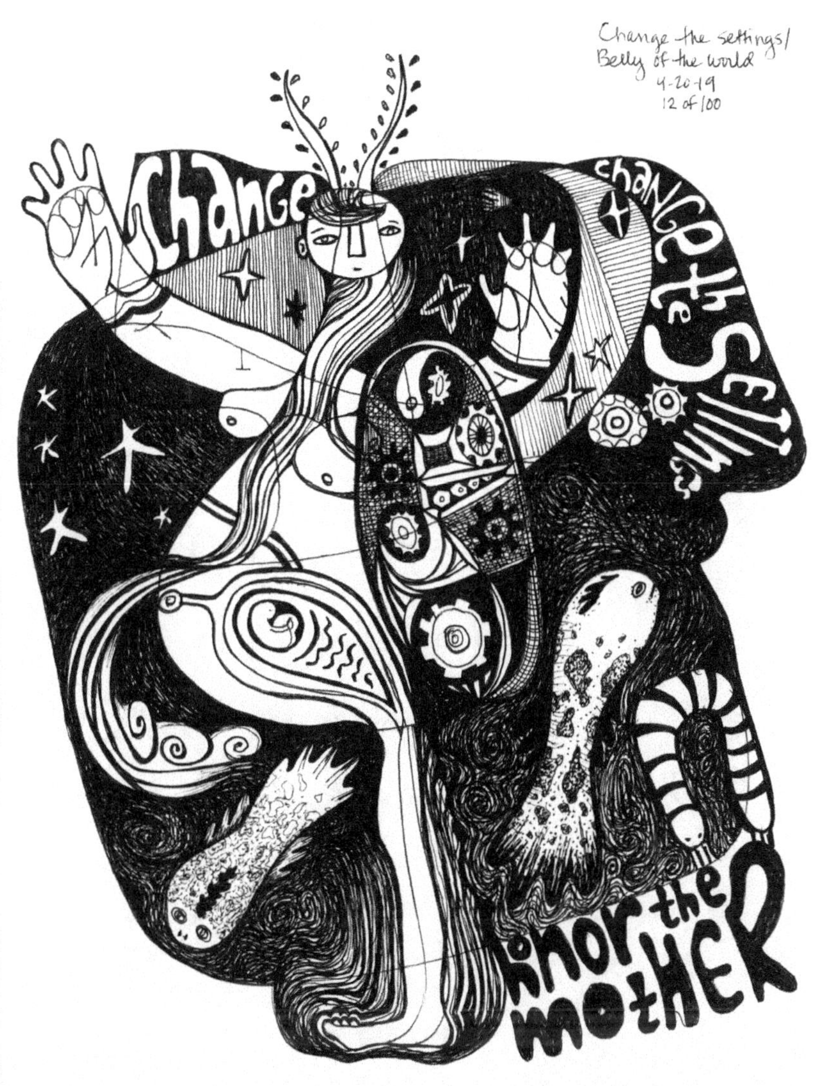

Change the settings/belly of the world (2019)

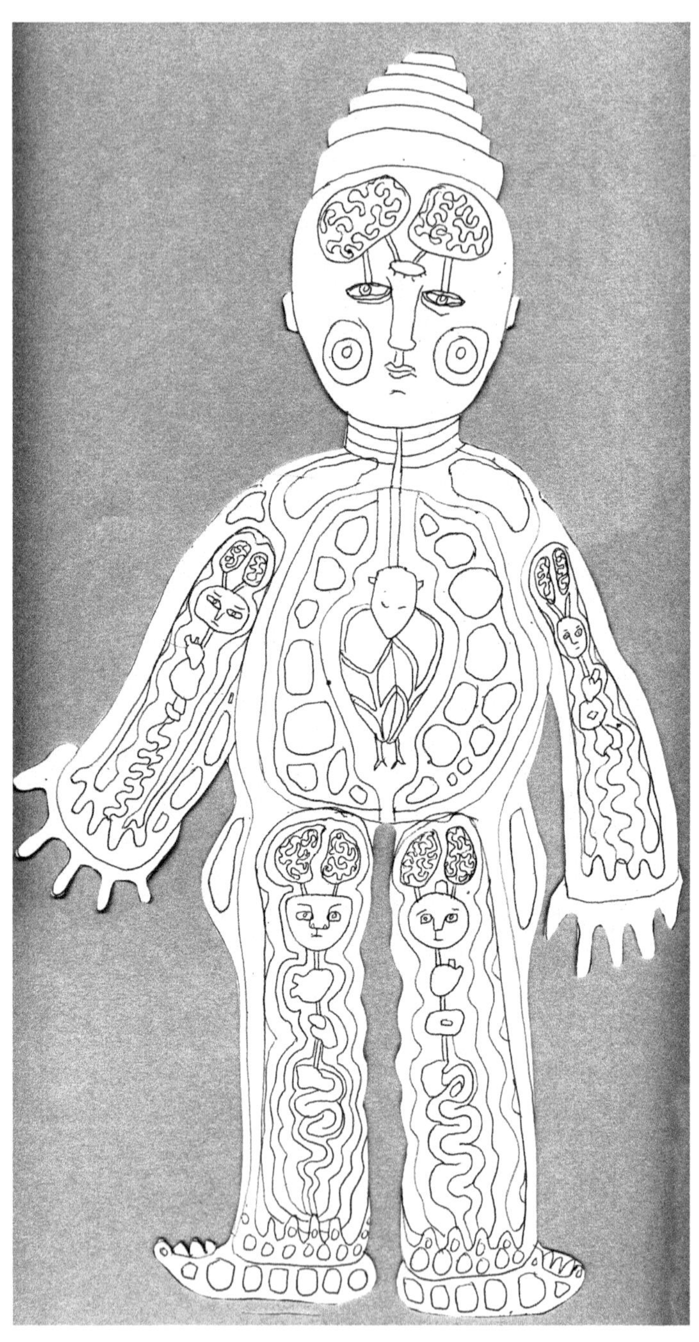

Visceral fat (2019)

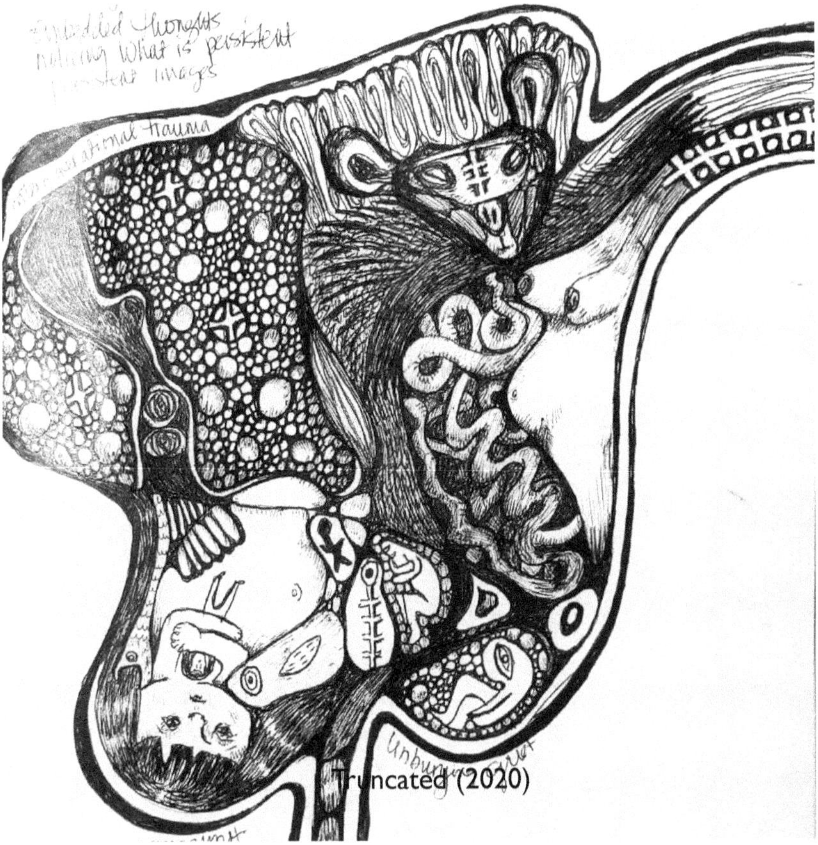

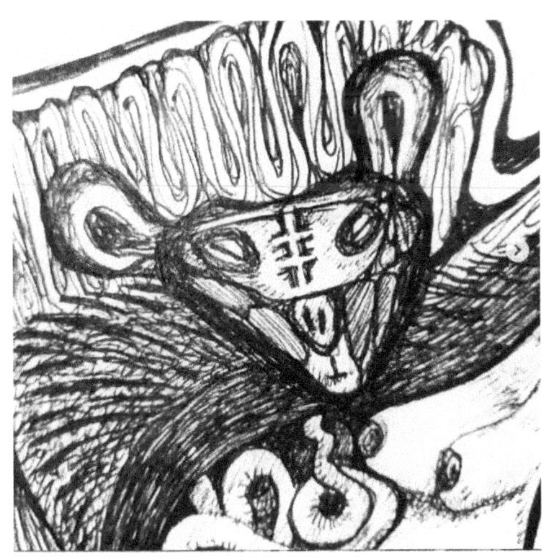

Truncated (2020)

detail

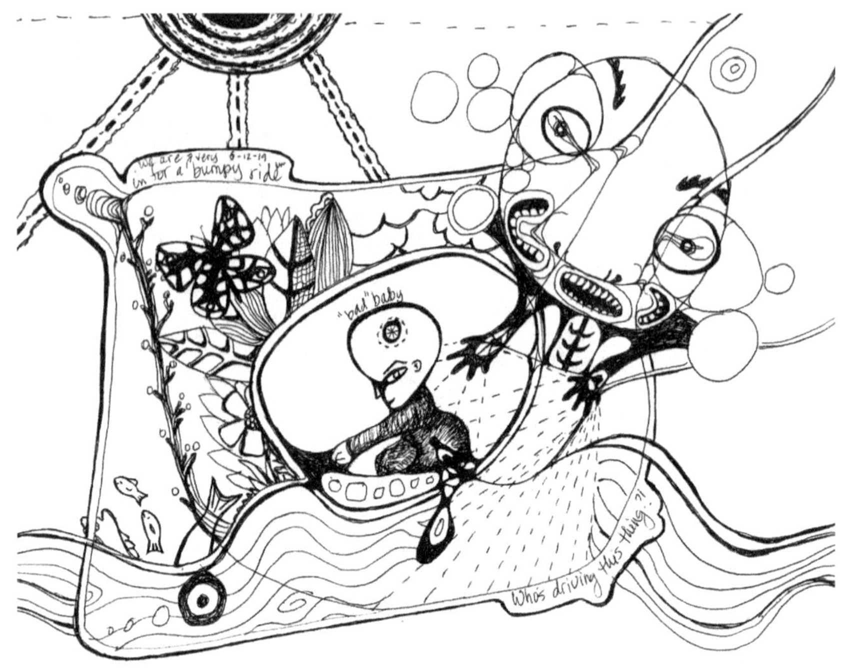

Who's driving this thing?!? (2019)

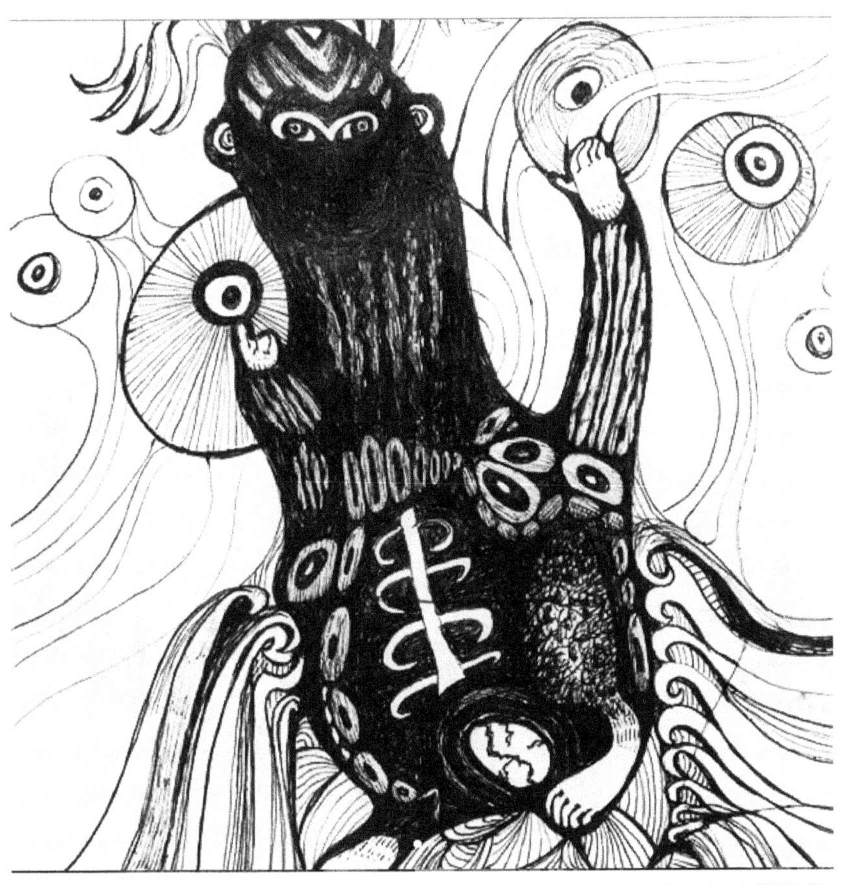

Untitled (2020)

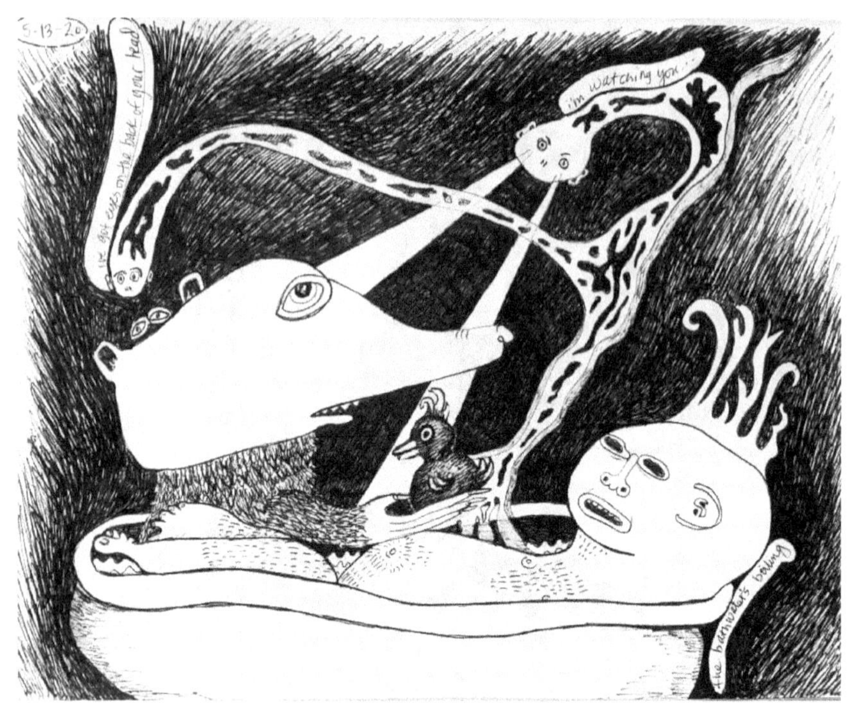

The Bathwater's Boiling (2020)

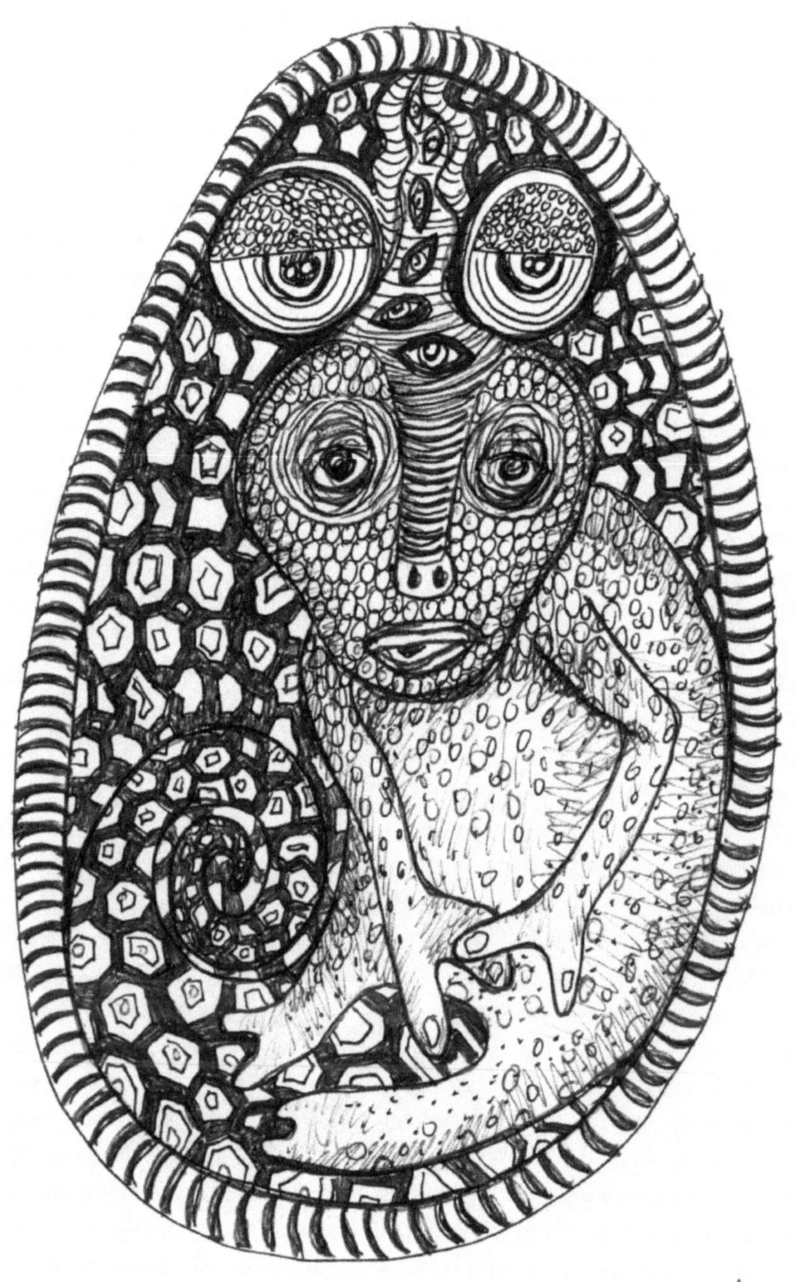

Wondrous alien birth (2021)

Blind Contour Drawings

Judith Hoffman

Judith Hoffman is a Portland-based book artist and artist-in-residence at the Zymoglyphic Museum. Her books are based on dreams, memories, and thoughts of death. To create the books, she combines collage, drawing, photography, and sometimes metalwork.

Judith's work can be seen at the following locations:

judithhoffman.net
 judithhoffman.blogspot.com
 @judehoffperson on Instagram

How to make a blind contour drawing

To make a blind contour drawing, my eye follows the contours of a face in a photograph while my hand with the pen draws that contour. I do not look at the paper. My goal is to produce a loose, wonky outline drawing that I can work on further while looking at the drawing and the source photo. I lift my hand when I need to. For example, after drawing the outline of the eyes and nose, I might lift my hand to start the face shape. Since some of my drawings are interesting and some are not, I like to quickly make 6 or 8 drawings in a row. Then I choose a few I want to work on further by adding hatching, patterns or collage. Sometimes I make the collage first and then draw on that.

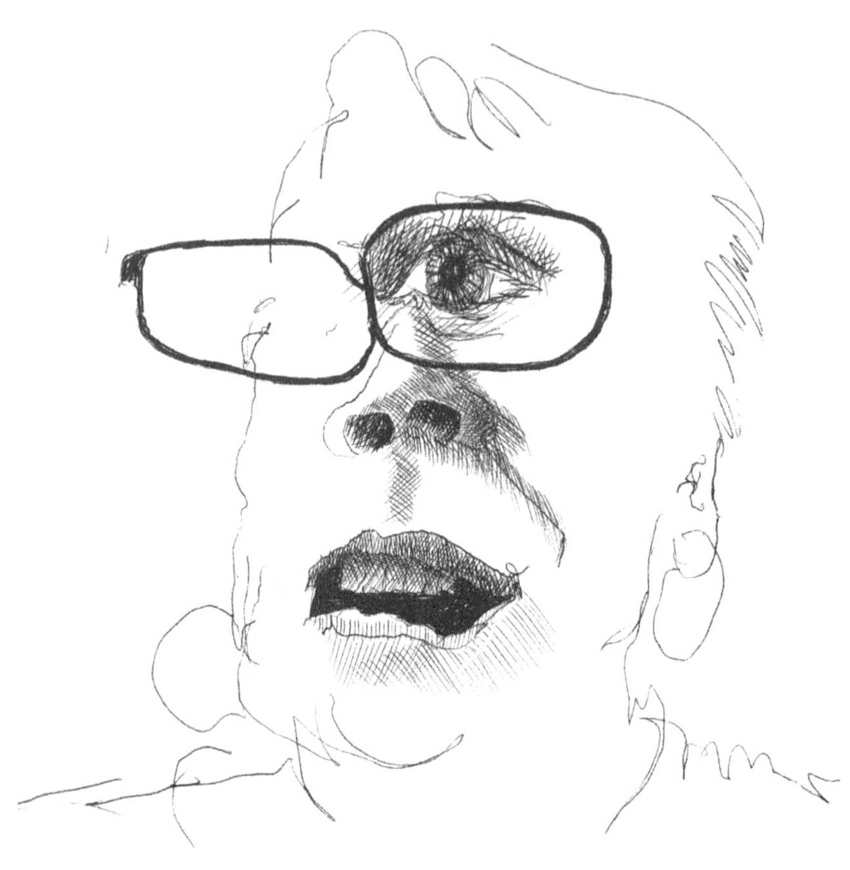

Eileen
June 6, 2020 – Pen drawing on paper, hatching added in Procreate on
iPad

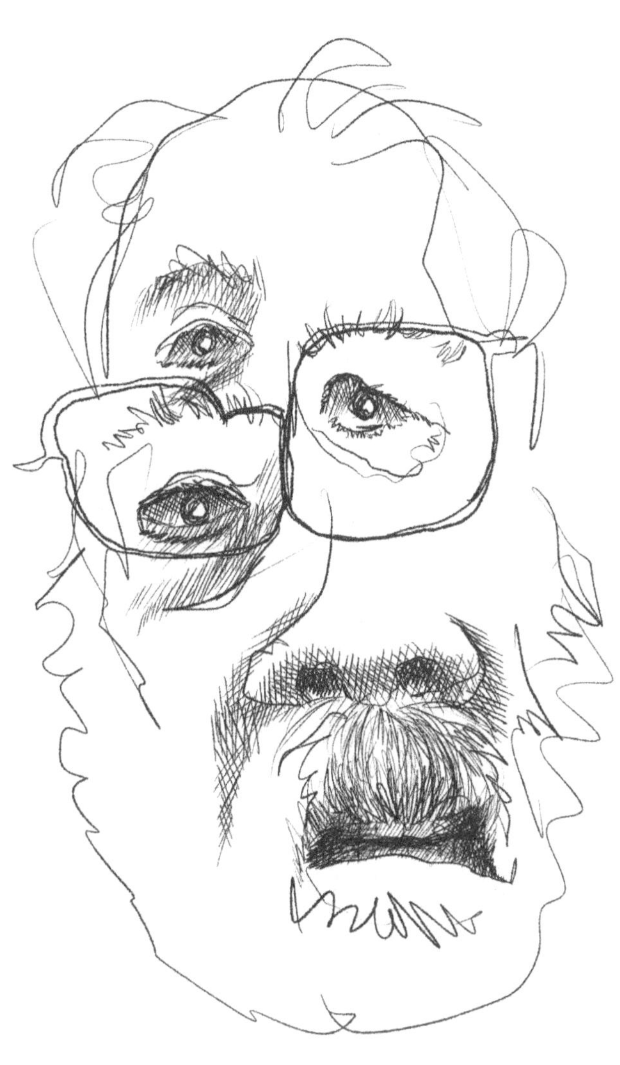

Jim with too many eyes
June 24, 2020 – Digital drawing done in Procreate on iPad

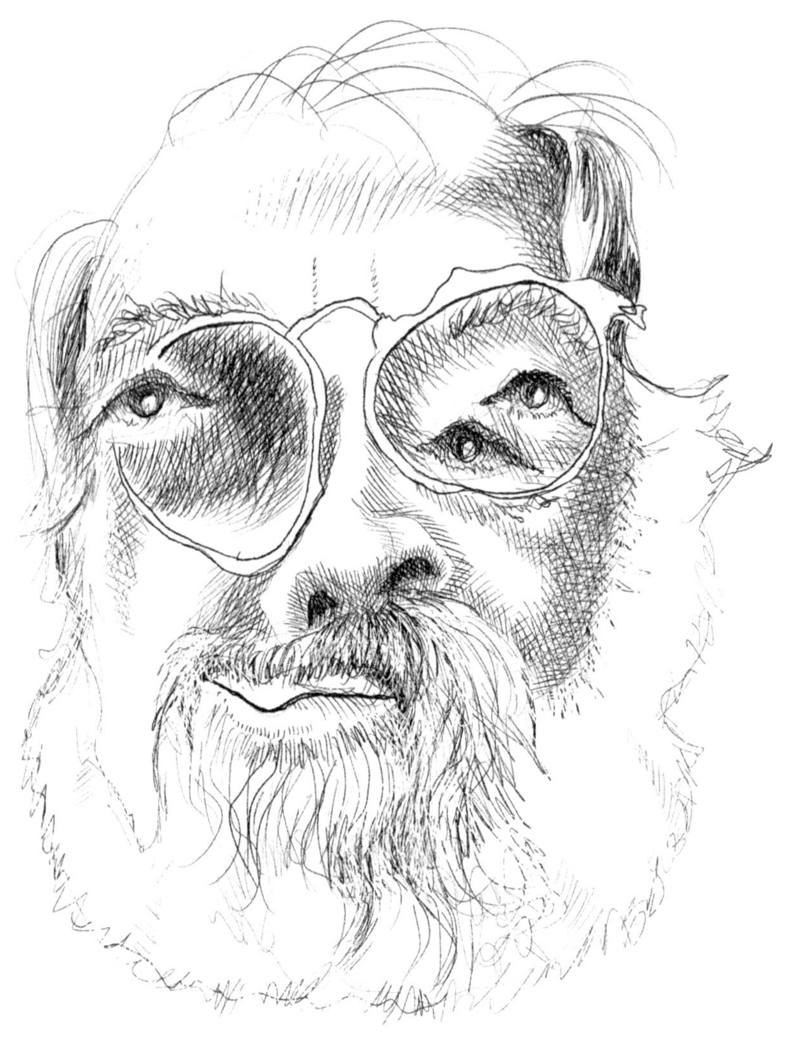

Jim
June 20, 2020 – Digital drawing done in Procreate on iPad

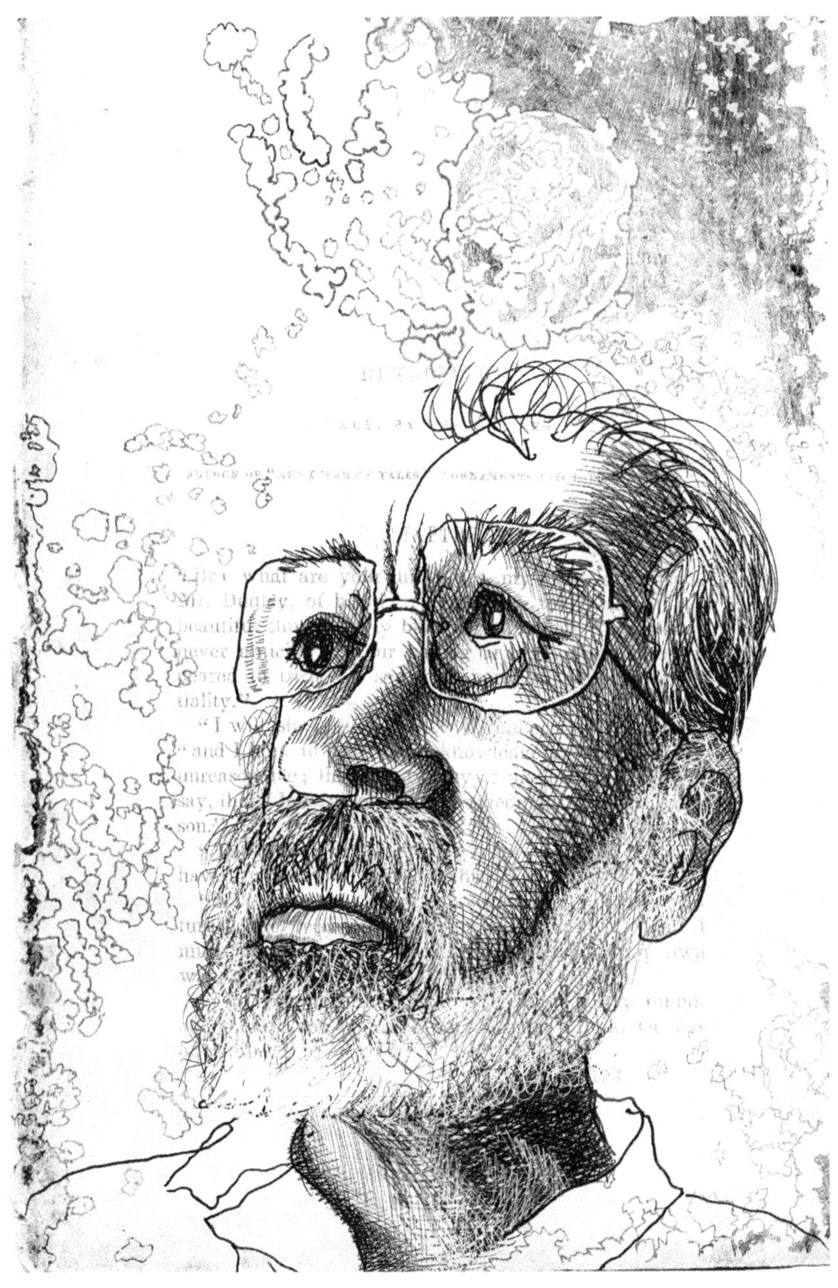

Jim on stained book page
June 19 2020 — Pen drawing on paper

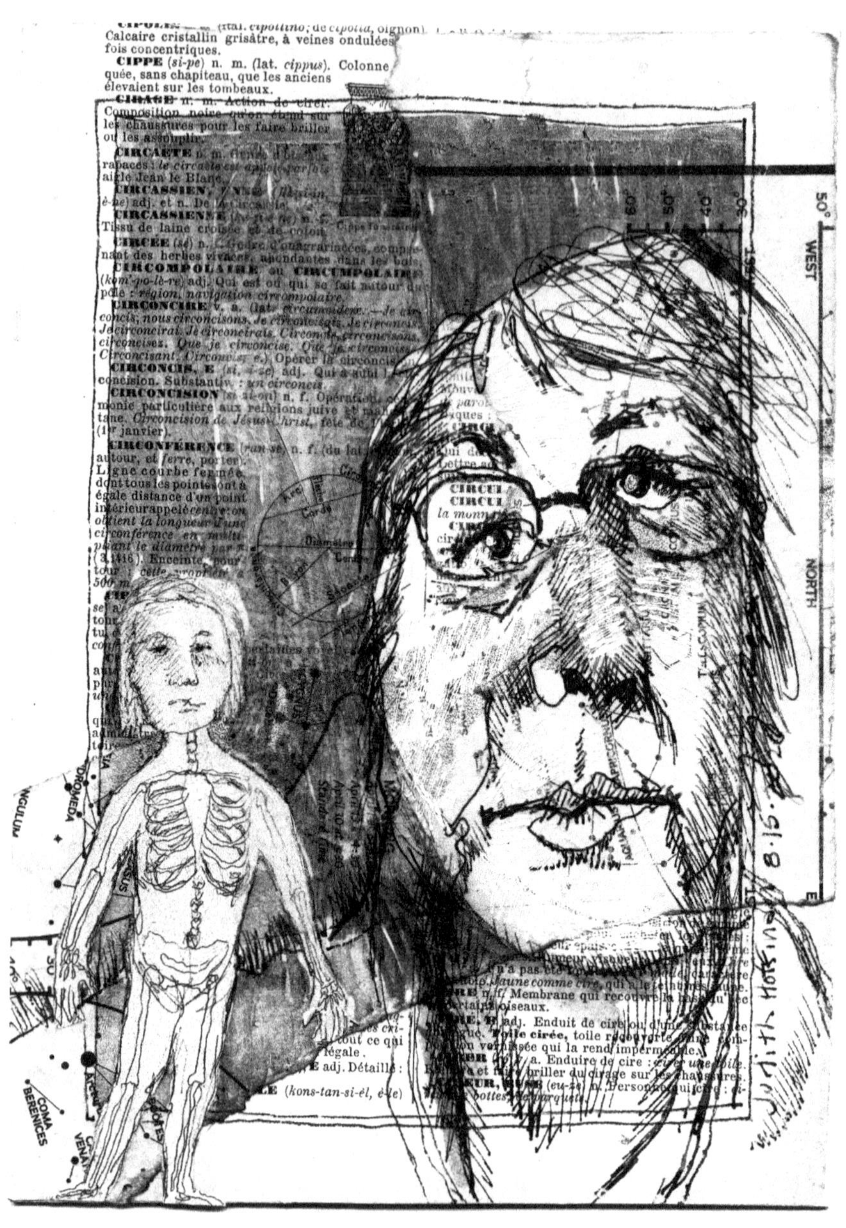

Jude with dream figure
August 20, 2020 — Pen drawing on collage

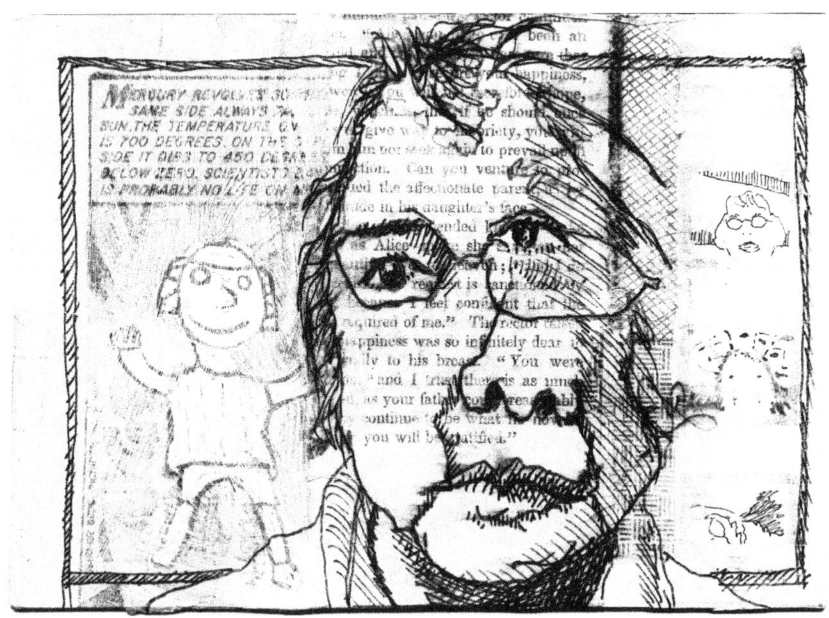

Look into the past
July 16, 2020 – Pen drawing on collage

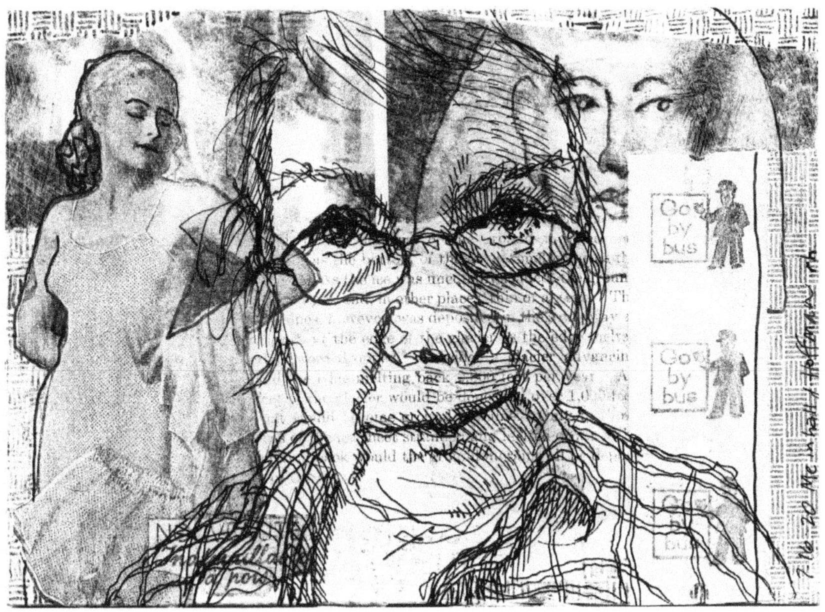

Ride the bus
July 16, 2020 – Pen drawing on collage

Pulverem Revertis

Amanda Quiroz

Amanda Quiroz is a Portland based artist. Inspired by her insect collection, she explores Catholic themes, primarily humility and mortality. Her contemplative drawings of insects and dust from the air seek to illuminate the invisible.

The works included here were shown in her solo show at the Zymoglyphic Museum's short-lived art gallery in the summer of 2016, titled "Pulverem Revertis" (dust to dust).

Her work is included in the Mount Angel Abbey Museum's permanent collection and may be viewed at amandaquiroz.com

I find, collect, and draw the minutiae from mundane interactions with nature. Focusing on overlooked objects typically categorized as dust: dried seeds, dead insects, fallen feathers, strands of hair. I combine these small forms to scale within accumulated compositions using ethereal abstraction inspired by early photomicroscopy and astrophotography. I am stimulated by this subject matter philosophically, as it leads to theological conversations. Scientific illustration, Italian Renaissance art, along with Catholicism, Sacred Liturgy, and divine phenomena all commingle in an undercurrent influencing my work. I'm drawn to harmonious parallels between the infinitesimal and the grandiose through my process.

—Amanda Quiroz

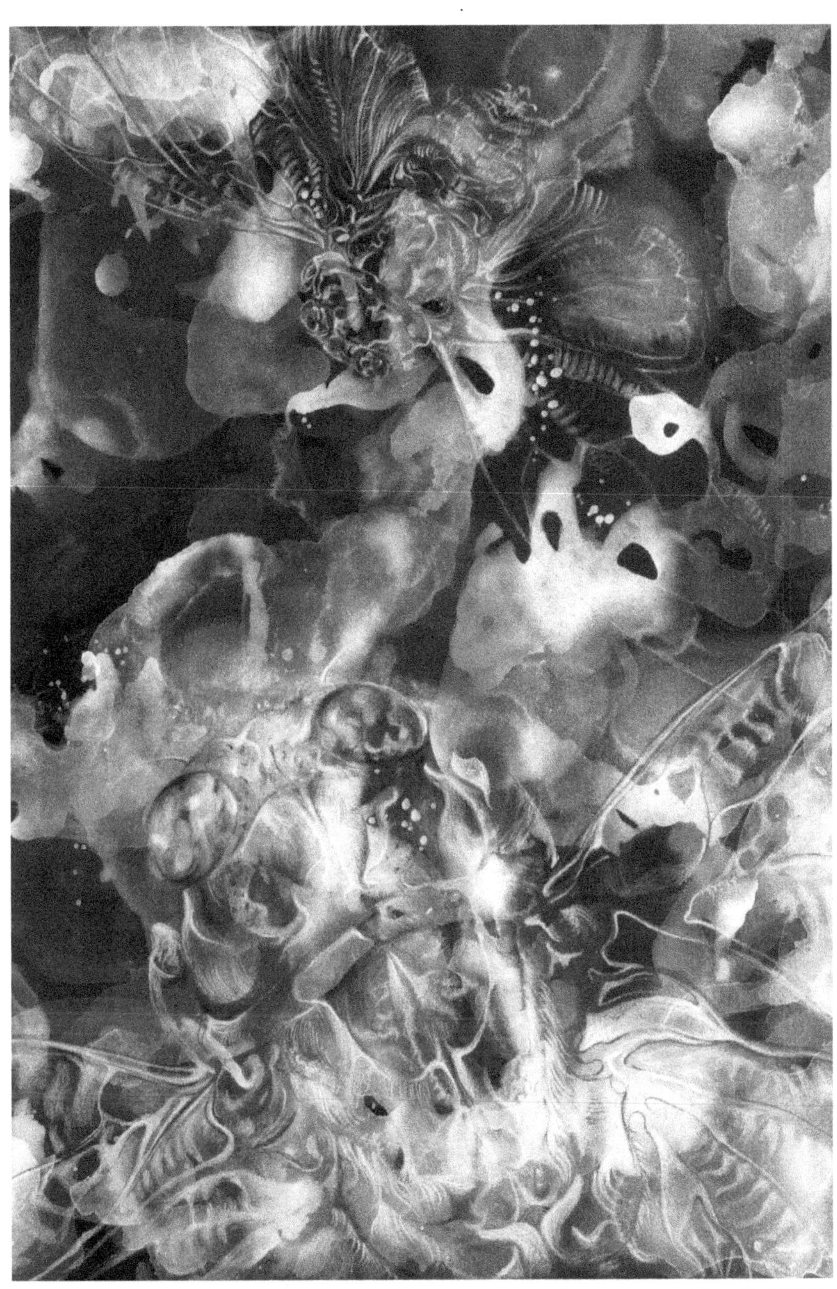

Reverence (detail, 2010)

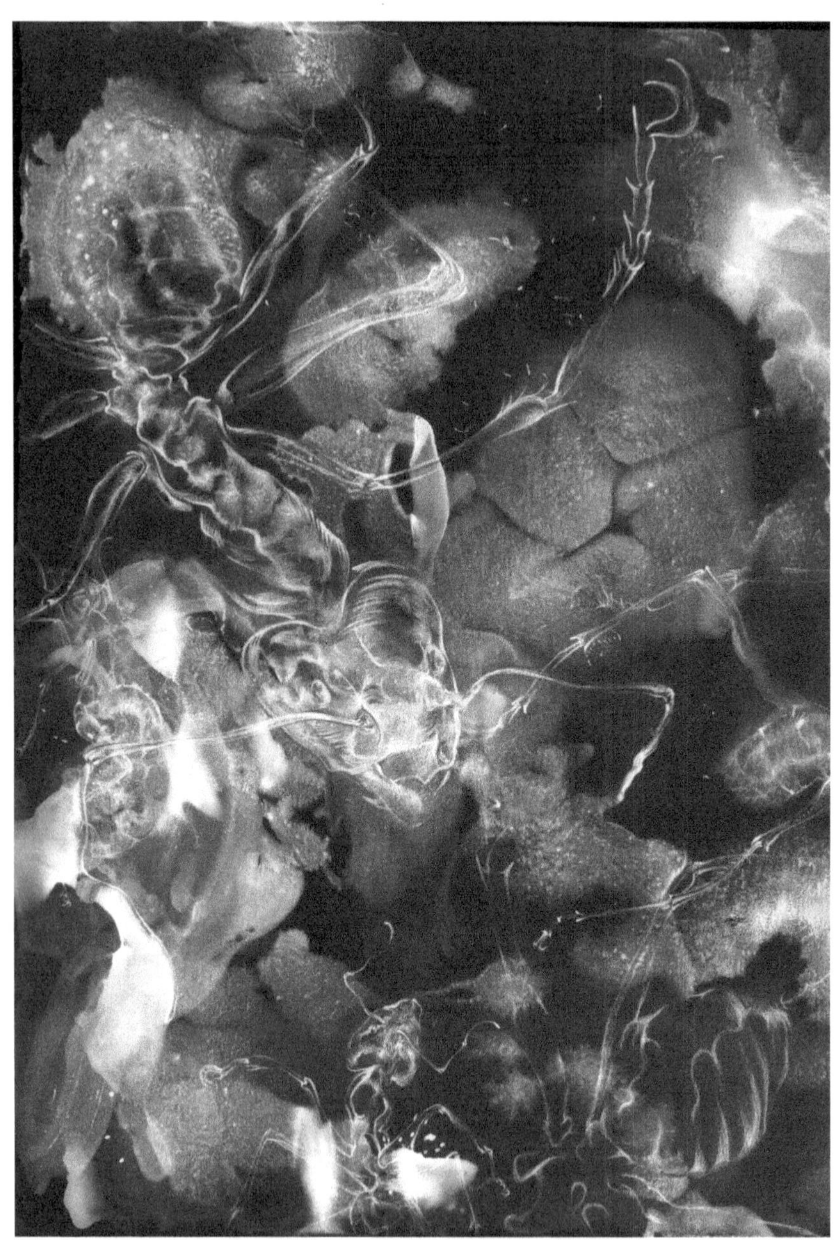

Deliverance (detail, 2010)

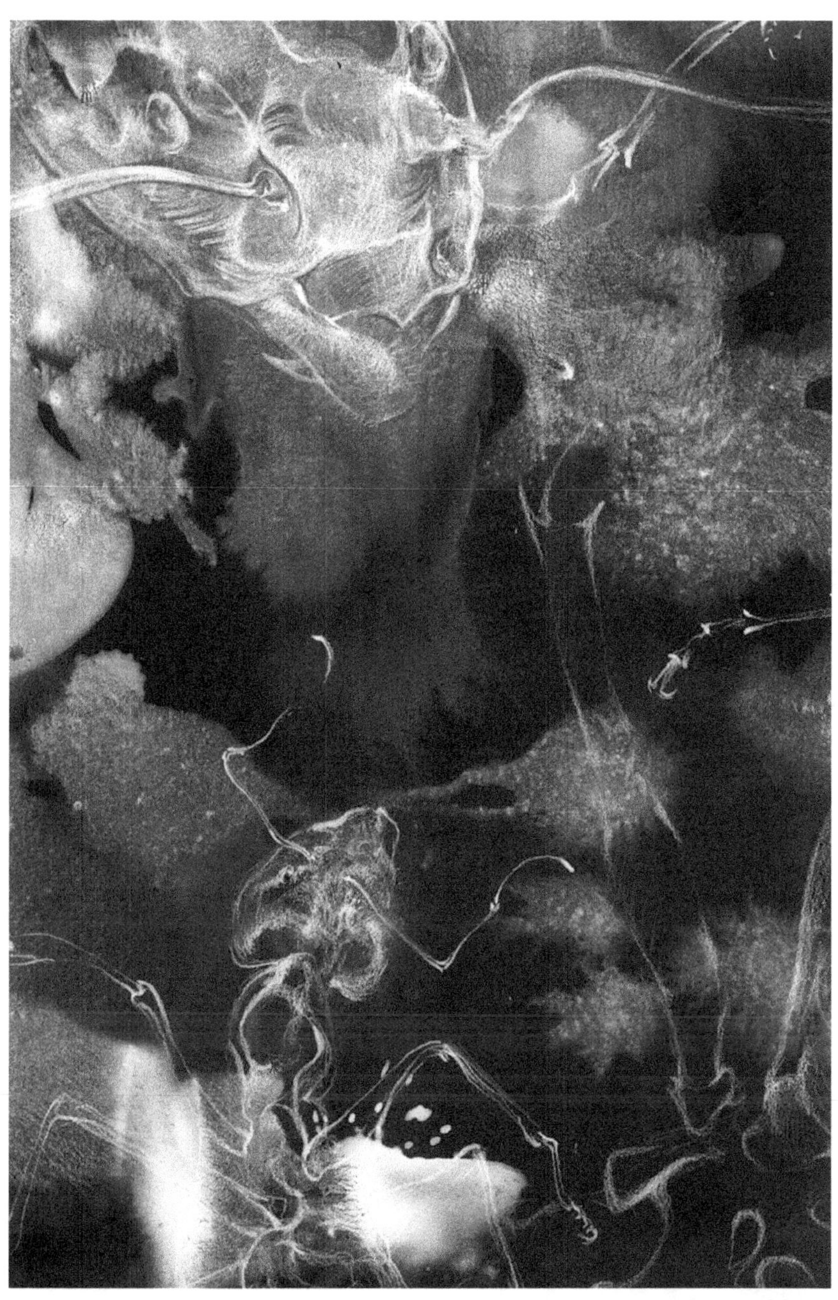

Deliverance (detail, 2010)

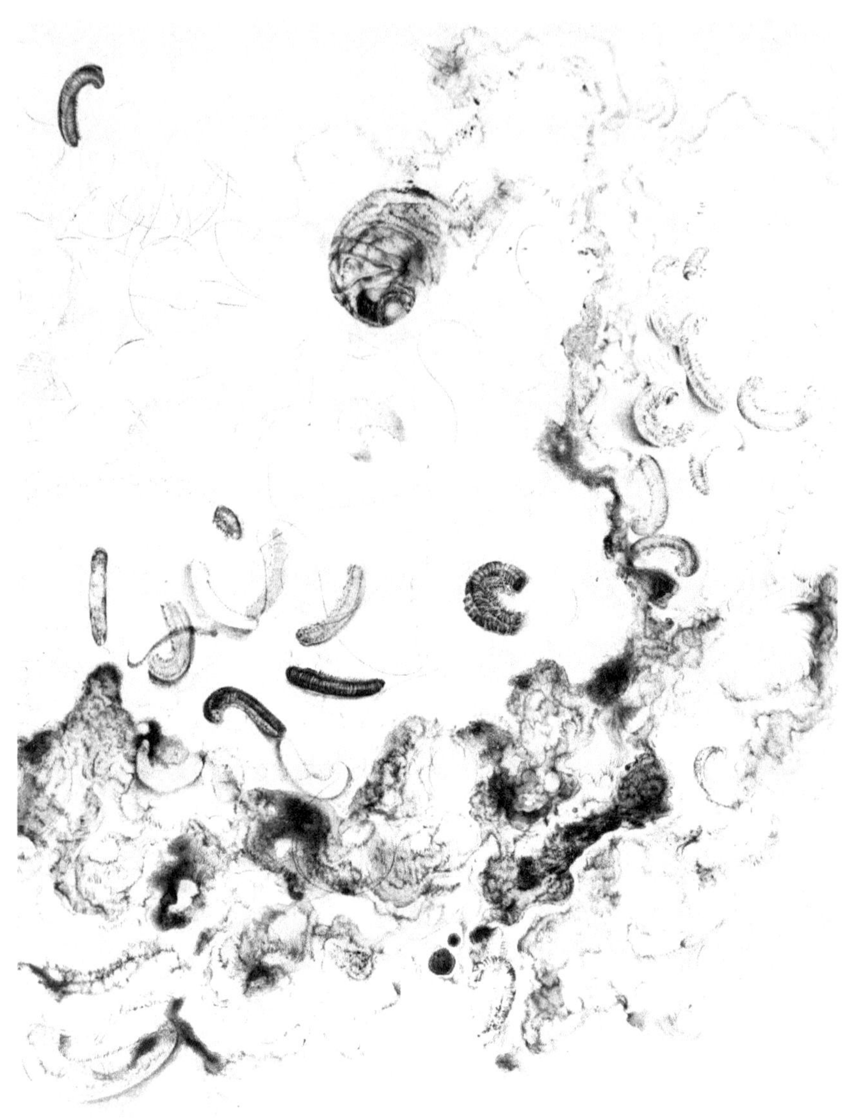

Dust Collection: Pulse - (detail, 2012)

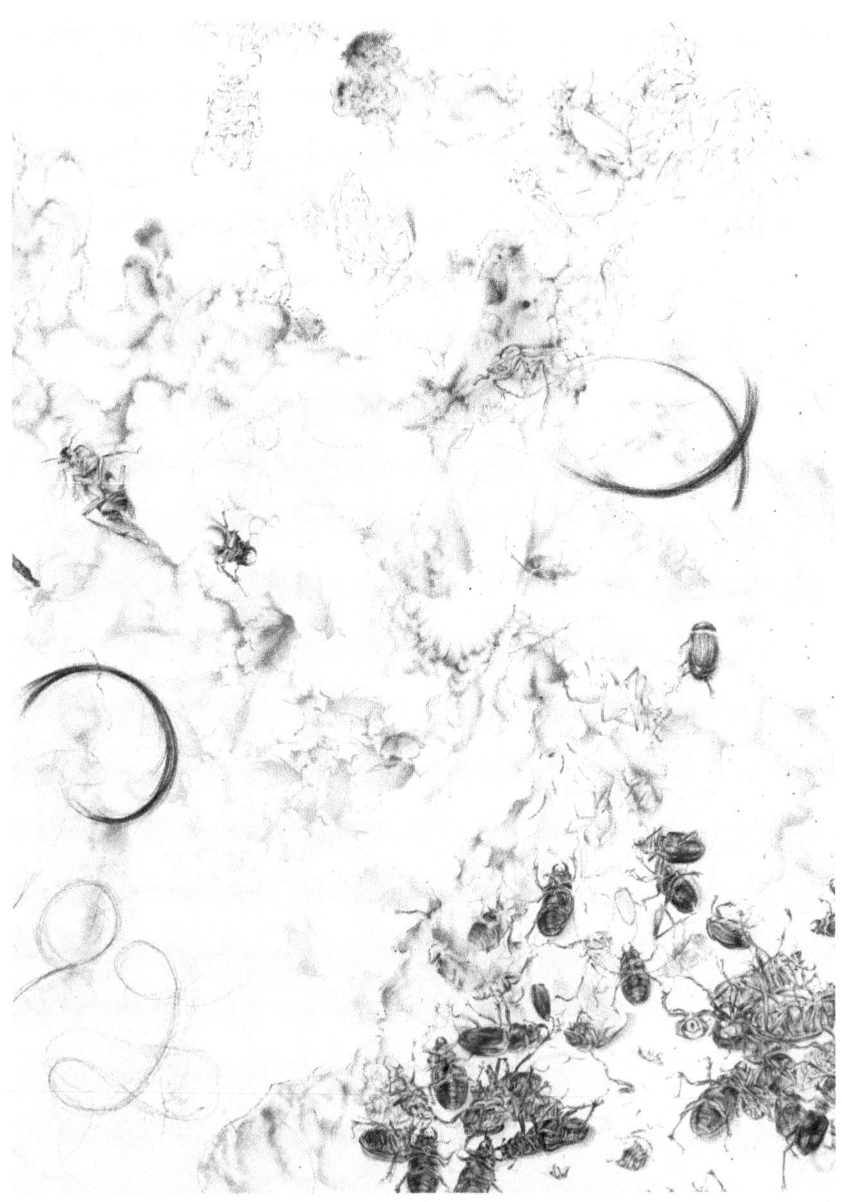

Dust Collection: Void I (detail, 2011)

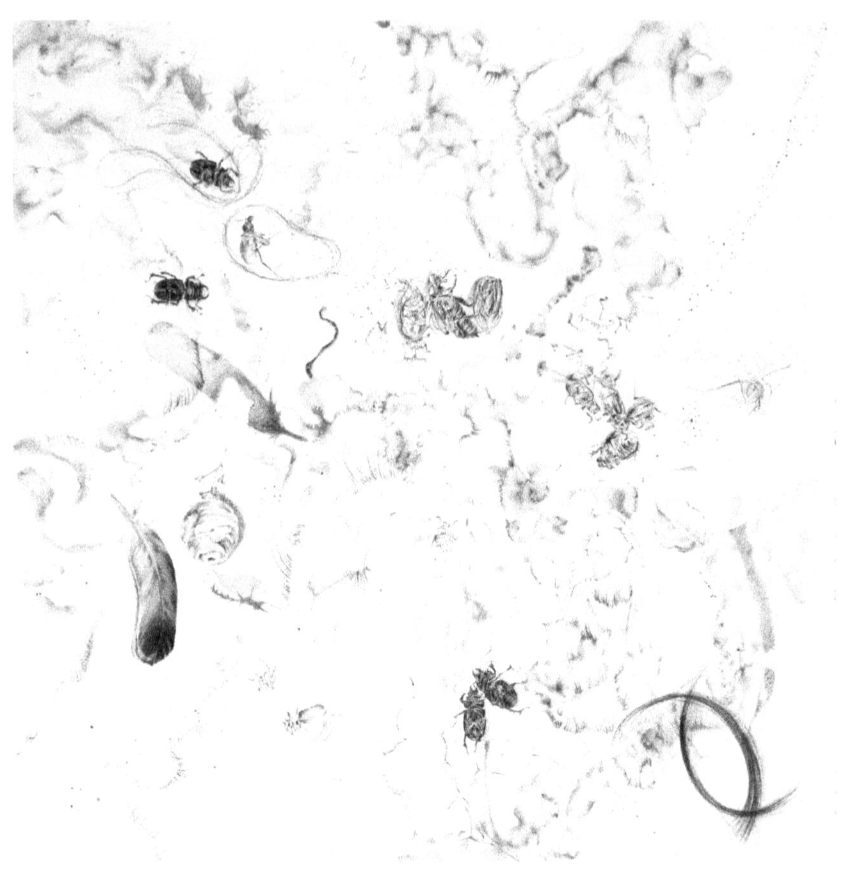

Dust Collection: Void II (2011)

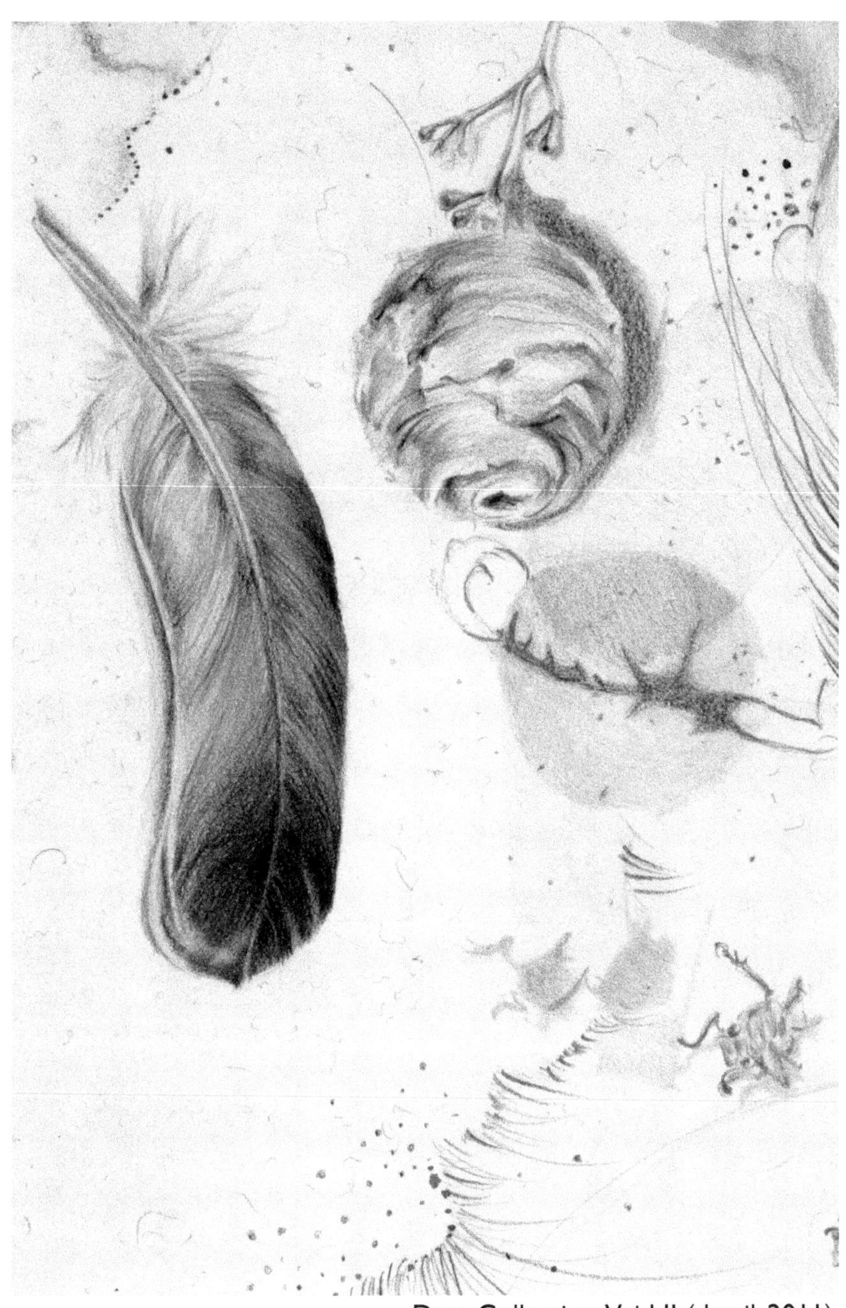

Dust Collection: Void II (detail, 2011)

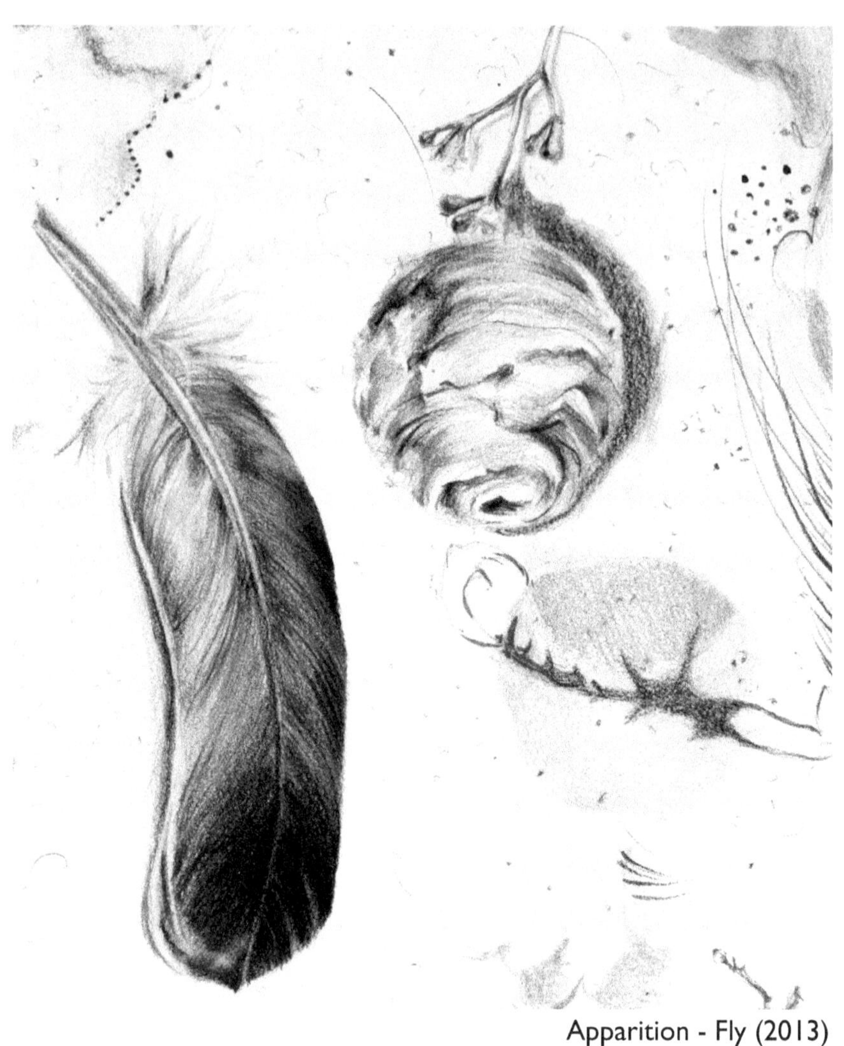

Apparition - Fly (2013)

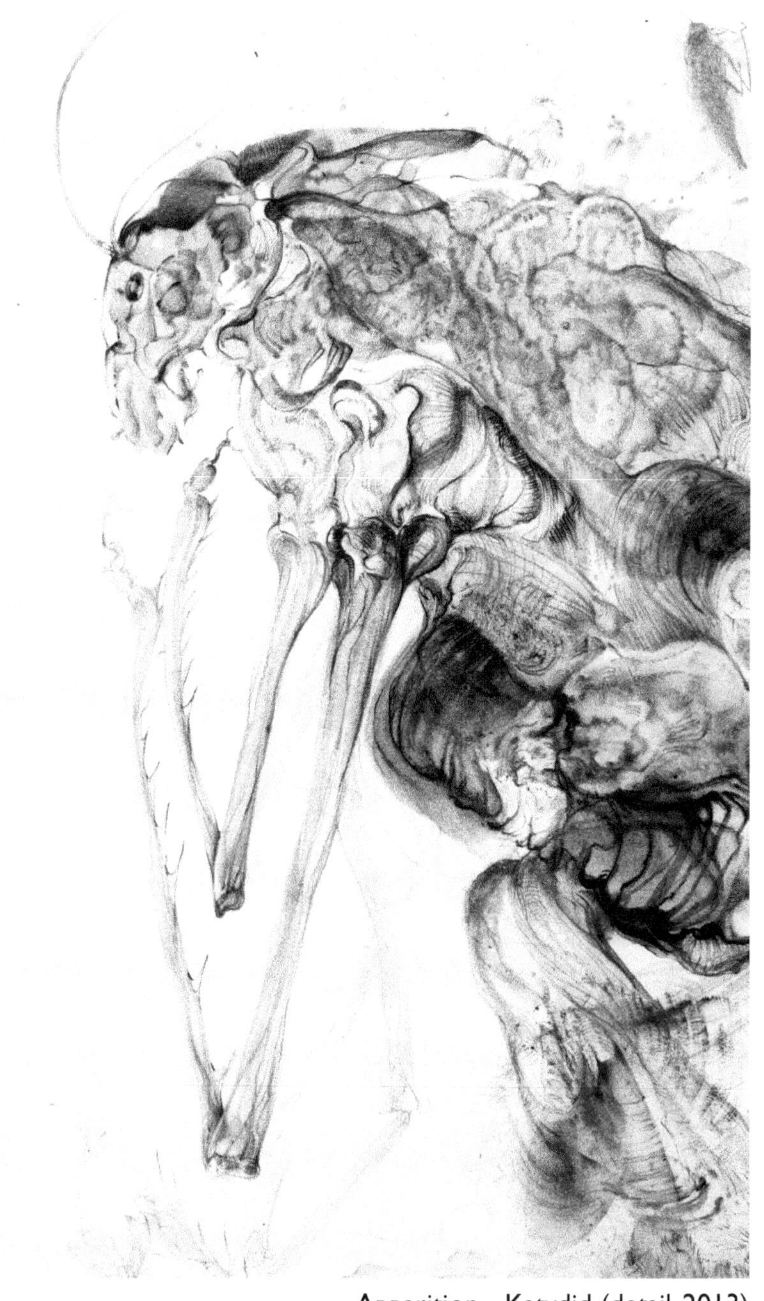

Apparition - Katydid (detail, 2013)

SIGNS AND ARTIFACTS FROM THE FAUX MUSEUM

Thomas Lucky Richards

Tom Richards is the curator and custodian emeritus of the Faux Museum. The museum was noted for its Great Woolly Ant, which currently resides in Zymoglyphic Museum.

Tom is the author of *Thirst for Beginners: Poems, Prose, Quizzes* (University of Hell Press, 2020)

The Faux Museum was a conceptual art museum that I ran for a year in 1991 and then again from 2012 to 2015, in the depths and dregs of Old Town Portland, Oregon. I was the curator/janitor of The Faux. I inherited the concept from my ancestors who started the first museum in a cave in what is now Alaska some 10,000 years ago after they crossed Beringia, the land bridge (primarily ice from what I was told).

I was inspired to lie to people so they could find out the truth. I wanted my museum to be big and bold and outrageous and shine a light on the hypocrisies of our societies. I wanted my museum to bring about critical thinking but with a laugh track. I had art and installations from all over the globe and it attracted patrons from all fifty states and over sixty different countries (possibly 61).

My favorite shows included: The Faux Masters (artists' takes on traditional master works), The Liars Hall of Shame, The Monument of the Seventh Dimension, and of course – the Faux University School Carnival Extravaganza Thing (which included The Road-Kill Petting Zoo).

—Tom Richards

COLLECTIONS & ANOMALIES : PUBLIC & PRIVATES

THE STATE OF THE WONDER

We at The Faux Museum have been contemplating wonder. For instance we were asking ourselves; where has it gone to? I see wonder as a beautiful and dreamy subset of curiosity. Perhaps wonder is a commodity like soy beans, or silver and it is currently not in high demand. If so we would like to free it from this commodified stricture. Wonder should be as free as oxygen. Wonder is a way of seeing life, the child's way, the artist's way. Wonder is a combination of a life-giving element such as oxygen mixed with the purest form of joy, fascination, awe and reverence. Wonder is a way of seeing. It is the poetic instructions of how life transpires and where we fit into it.

The Faux Museum has gathered a disparate collection of collections and anomalies. We humans are collectors, but we are not alone. One of my favorite collectors in this world is the Satin Bowerbird of Australia. The male Satin Bowerbird builds a structure of sticks which is called a bower. In front of this archway-like structure is a small field in which the male has collected and arranged found objects most of which are bluish. These objects vary widely from berries and flowers to manmade objects such as bits of plastic, buttons or whatever the mating bird feels fits in aesthetically. The bowers and presentation are truly wondrous. We hope the objects and collections which we have chosen to exhibit here will make you happy today and inspire your wonder for the beauty in the seemingly ordinary of our fascinating world.

Thank you.

Tom Richards
Curator/Janitor

Special Guest Co-Curator from the Tiny Museum Wendy Giesler

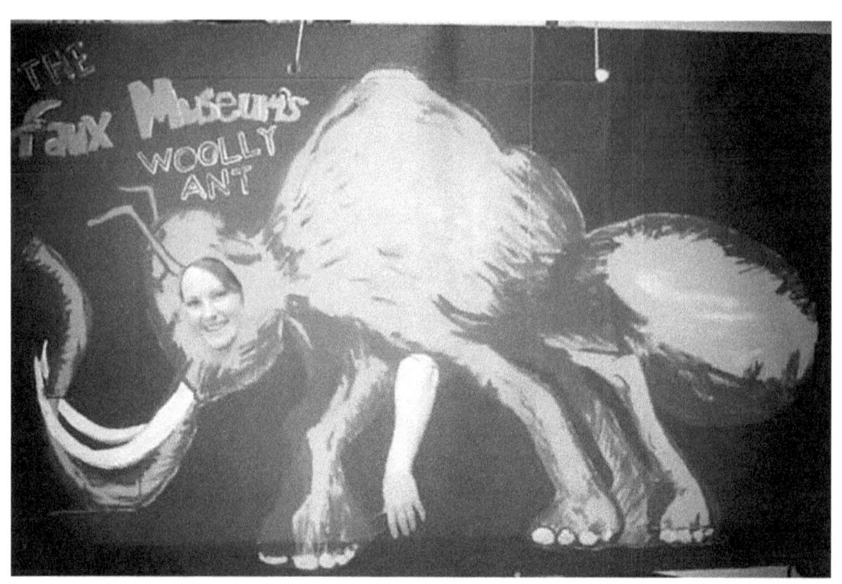

THE
faux Museum's
WOOLLY
ANT

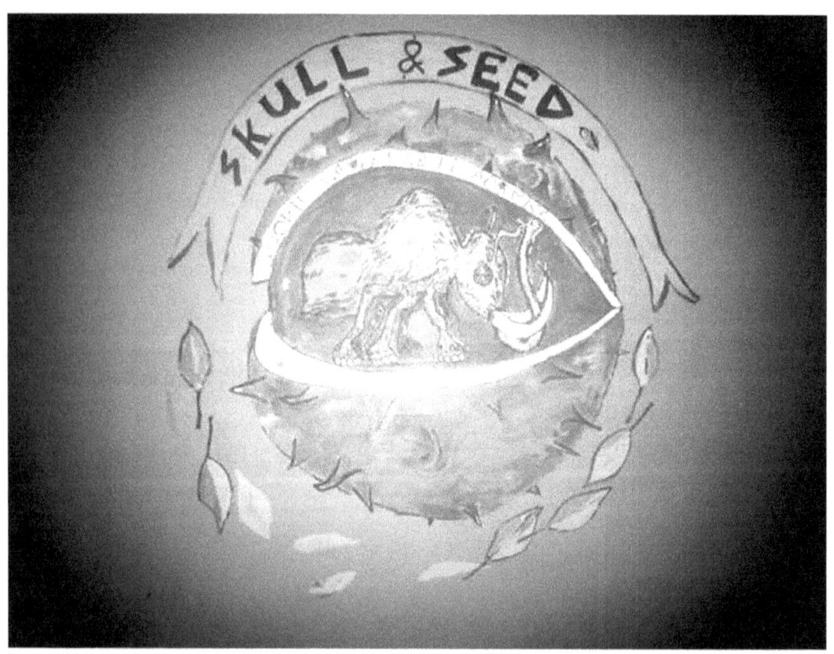

SKULL & SEED

The Great Woolly Ant

Kingdom Animalia – Animals

Phylum Arthropoda – arthropods

Subphylum Hexapoda – hexapods

Class Insecta – hexapoda, insects

Subclass Pterygota –winged insects

Infraclass Neoptera – modern, wing-folding insects

Order Hymenoptera –ants, bees, wasps

Suborder Apocrita –ants, bees, narrow-waisted hymenopterans, true wasps

Infraorder Aculeata

Superfamily Vespoidea – vespoid wasps

Family Mutillidae – velvet ants

Genus *Pilomutilla* Ruedas, L. 1899

The velvet ant family is the woolly ants closest living relative. They have wings but are flightless and are more wasps than ants even though that is their appearance. They were classified by the great anthropologist/ paleontologist/biologist/museologist Luis Ruedas in 1899.

There were many animals near Ug Faux's first Faux Museum site. There were Woolly Mammoths, Woolly Rhinoceros, Giant Sloths, Saber Toothed Tigers, Reindeer, Giant Beavers, the oft overlooked Dwarf Grizzly (a dogged six inch replica of today's fierce Alaskan bear) and many other unique animals. Ug Faux was the first homo sapien to domesticate an animal. He found the large hairy arthropods adorable and funny and so he began to train them, he eventually even harnessed several of them to his sled for transport. This very large member of the Formicidae family has come to be known today as the Woolly Ant.

The Origin of the Faux Museum

The Faux family began the museum tradition over ten thousand years ago. The Faux Museum was the first museum in the world and among its so called peers it is by far the oldest. Approximately ten thousand years ago the Faux family, after a trek across Asia and Siberia, crossed the Beringia land bridge and reached what is now the American state of Alaska. Within a few years of their arrival Ug Faux was born. Ug, who wore only black furs, eventually opened the first Faux Museum in a cave next to their igloo hut near present day Nenana. Nenana is just over a hundred miles west of Fairbanks and thirty miles north of Clear. All are presently connected by Highway US A-3. The museum's location was actually north of Nenana where present day North Nenana on the Tanana River on the Parks Highway where that oversized yellow Quonset hut house is. It's for sale now for $210,000 but I'm pretty sure they'll take $185,000, $190,000 or even less for cash.

The last 500,000 years of life on earth during the Cenozoic Era are known as the Quaternary Period. The Quaternary Period is divided into two epochs. The first 490,000 years of the Quaternary Period are known as the Pleistocene, or glacial epoch. The most recent ten or eleven thousand years are known as the Holocene epoch. Most of the history of the Faux museum can be found in the Holocene, but the origins of the Faux museum curatorial family began at the end of the Pleistocene in what is now the island country of Ireland.

During this time, due to the massive glaciation of the northern continents, the ocean levels were quite a bit lower and many of the islands of today were connected to other land masses. The islands of the United Kingdom were thus attached to present day Europe at the time. According to legend O. Faux and his family were persuaded to travel eastward out of Ireland through what is now England and over the continent by a group of irate clansmen carrying stones and flinging threats and insults serious enough for the Fauxs to rest only after they had crossed the Himalayan mountains (which were considerably shorter at the time). In a

village which is now known as Kashi, O Faux was struck by
a stone in the head and perished. The grievance of the rock
throwing clansmen is no longer known but they left Lady Faux
unharmed and returned to their homes as they were. Lady Faux
was taken in by the locals who were traveling northeast following
the migrating mammoths and mastodons. As it turned out Lady
Faux was with child and after only a few full moons Ada Faux
was born. Ada and Lady Faux lived with these tribesmen as
the continued northeast for what we think now must have been
several decades.

When they reached the end of the Siberian peninsula where
today we find the Bering Straight they found Beringia (which
of course is our modern name derived from the great explorer
Bering.) They did not find water there instead they found a
land bridge at least sixty miles wide. This land bridge was
made possible by the impediment they were soon to discover.
As previously stated glaciers covered much of the earth. All of
Canada and some of America were covered with glaciers up
to two miles thick. Up to 30% of the land mass of the earth
was covered by glaciers at time. All of these enormous glaciers
held huge amounts of water lowering the ocean levels and thus
opening land bridges such as Beringia and the one that allowed
O Faux to flee from England to Europe without getting his
moccasins wet.

When Ada and his mother reached present day Alaska they
built a home while waiting for the glaciers to melt. Lady Faux
encouraged Ada over and over and over to take a mate or else
no one would have him at his advanced age. Ada finally gave in
and shacked up with Snow and soon Ug Faux was born. Ada had
become an incomparable hunter and was killing large mammals
such as mastodons, woolly mammoths, giant sloths, and Bison,
among other large mammals. Gradually the glaciers began to
recede and shrink and about 10,000 or 11,000 years ago some
of the bison slipped between the slowly retreating Cordilleran
ice sheet and the larger Laurentide glacier to the east. These
ice sheets had covered the entirety of Canada on down into the

northern regions of the United States. The ice was up to two miles thick in the north and slipped well into the Midwest far south of Chicago*.

*Residents of present day Chicago would barely recognize this frozen, yet less windy, minitropolis.

D: Your faux history actually has a really strong real history backbone.

TR: Right, it does. I try to do that with everything because the museum is actually a critical thinking museum. It's a conceptual art museum of course, but it's a critical thinking museum with a sense of humor. So I tried to put as much truth in as I can. But every day people question if it's real.

D: That is interesting because in all museums, all the information is just an interpretation, visitors should think critically about what is presented.

TR: Exactly, and not just in museums but everything and that's what I would like to get visitors to do. When someone is "dumb" and asks if there was really a Woolly Ant, I really love that. Some people don't know they shouldn't ask that. Then there are people who are too cool to ask questions, even if they are not sure. Someone wrote that the exhibition had holes in it, that it wasn't finished very well. But they just didn't get the concept of the idea of a set, like a play or opera.

D: Going through the museum, I had initially thought you were a writer.

TR: I used to write about art...Art is the thought that you put into it that is just as important as the other part. In fact you can have all thought and nothing else. So I think that writing is important, or at least thinking about writing.

Interview with Duplex Gallery, June 26, 2013

End Notes

Credits

Book title text treatment by Gigi Little (gigilittle.com)

Cover art by Jim Stewart based on eco-dye print by Judith Hoffman and engravings from Ernst Haeckel's *Die Radiolarien* (1862, reprinted by Prestel Verlag as *Art Forms from the Ocean*, 2005)

Text and image on page 4 by Coleman Stevenson, from *Meditations on the Alchemical Journey*

Collages on page 7 and page 62 by Jim Stewart from *Views of the Zymoglyphic Region*

Drawing of museum building on page 15 by Judith Hoffman

More from the Zymoglyphic Museum Press

Oneiric Memoir by Jason Squamata (2020)
The Zymoglyphic Museum: A Guide to the Exhibits (2020)
The Zymoglyphic Anthology (2019)
Hotel Zymoglyphic by Jason Squamata (2019)
Views of the Zymoglyphic Region (2011)
Sketches of the Zymoglyphic Region (2010)

See **zymoglyphic.org/pubs.html** for details